*Law*Basics

CRIMINAL LAW

AUSTRALIA
Law Book Co.
Sydney

CANADA and USA
Carswell
Toronto

HONG KONG
Sweet & Maxwell Asia

NEW ZEALAND
Brookers
Wellington

SINGAPORE and MALAYSIA
Sweet & Maxwell Asia
Singapore and Kuala Lumpur

*Law*Basics

CRIMINAL LAW

By

Clare Connelly, M.A. (HONS), LL.B., DIP.L.P.

Solicitor
Senior Lecturer, School of Law, University of Glasgow

EDINBURGH
W. GREEN/Sweet & Maxwell
2002

Published in 2002 by

W. Green & Son Ltd
21 Alva Street
Edinburgh EH2 4PS

www.wgreen.co.uk

Printed and Bound in Great Britain by Athenaeum Press Ltd,
Gateshead, Tyne & Wear

No natural forests were destroyed to make this product;
Only farmed timber was used and replanted

A CIP catalogue record for this book is available from the British
Library

ISBN 0414 012 313

CONTENTS

TABLE OF CASES

1. INTRODUCTION

Criminal law in the broadest sense incorporates the rules of procedure and substantive criminal law. Rules of procedure govern how cases are progressed through court and substantive criminal law defines crimes and defences. Scottish criminal law is predominantly common law. Common law refers to law that does not stem from a statute and is laid down in authoritative writings and judicial decisions. The substantial body of common law in Scotland is supplemented by some statutes, including, the Misuse of Drugs Act 1976 and the Road Traffic Act 1984. This text is concerned primarily with the common law element of Scottish criminal law.

PROSECUTION

There is a system of public prosecution in Scotland. Private prosecutions are permissible but only under restricted conditions and are very rare. In a public prosecution, the prosecution is brought at the instance of the Lord Advocate in the High Court and at the instance of the Procurator Fiscal in the sheriff or district courts. The decisions regarding whether a prosecution should be brought, the crime(s) to be charged, the court and form of proceeding are made by procurators fiscal depute and this process is called "marking". Decisions regarding prosecution cannot be reviewed by the public.

Trials proceed on an indictment in solemn cases and a complaint in summary cases. The charge in an indictment is sometimes called "a libel". Both indictments and complaints contain a statement of the crimes that are to be prosecuted. Cases are differentiated by whether or not a jury is present. Hence, in summary cases, where the charges will involve less serious crimes, a jury is not present and such trials take place in the sheriff or district courts. In solemn cases, the charges will involve more serious crimes, a jury is present and the trial will take place in either the sheriff court or the High Court.

Fifteen people serve on a jury and the verdict is by majority. Before a person can be convicted of a crime, at least eight of the 15 jurors must find the accused guilty. Scotland has three verdicts: guilty, not guilty and not proven. Contrary to popular belief, the not proven verdict has the same legal consequences as a not guilty verdict. The principle of *res judicata* applies equally to a person acquitted on a not guilty verdict as it does to a not proven verdict. *Res judicata* means "a case or matter decided". The effect of this rule is that following a verdict in a trial or where the prosecution have deserted a trial, no further prosecutions can be initiated against the accused on the same charges.

ACCUSED

The administration of criminal justice has a protective function in respect of the accused. In some reported cases, particularly older cases, the accused is sometimes referred to as the panel. The system therefore embodies the principles of the presumption of innocence, the right to a fair trial, rules of evidence, the availability of legal aid and *res judicata*. The onus of proof is always on the prosecution, to prove criminal responsibility beyond reasonable doubt. The exception to this is where the defence of insanity or diminished responsibility is pled which results in the onus switching to the defence, who require to prove on the balance of probability that the accused was suffering from insanity or diminished responsibility.

The age of criminal responsibility in Scotland is eight, however, at the time of writing, the Scottish Law Commission has issued a "Discussion Paper on [the] Age of Criminal Responsibility" (Paper No. 115), which may result in change. This review has, in part, been instigated in order to determine whether the existing provisions of Scots law are in breach of the European Convention on Human Rights (hereinafter referred to as "the Convention"). Since the establishment of the Scottish Parliament in July 1999, under the authority of the Scotland Act 1998, neither the Parliament nor the Scottish Executive, which the Lord Advocate is a member of, can act in any way that is incompatible with the rights embodied in the Convention. This means that the criminal courts in Scotland must not contravene the terms of the Convention. Certain areas of law are reserved to the Westminster Parliament including, drugs, road traffic and offensive weapons. The requirement for the criminal law and courts to comply with the Convention has so far affected procedural rather than substantive issues of criminal law. One area where there may be difficulties is in relation to the amendment of existing crimes or the introduction of new crimes.

DEVELOPMENT OF CRIMINAL LAW

Scottish criminal law is regarded by many as a flexible system as it is almost exclusively common law and is based on existing principles that have evolved through judicial decisions. It does not comprise either a criminal code or statutes in respect of the majority of crimes. But if we do not have a statutory system how do we create new crimes or amend existing crimes?

The High Court of Justiciary is regarded as having an "inherent power" to declare the common law. This power is called the "declaratory power". This power was described by Hume as the "inherent power to punish every act which is obviously of a criminal nature" (i, 12). This power is only exercisable by a quorum of at least three judges in the High Court of Justiciary. The last explicit use of the power was in *Bernard Greenhuff* (1838) when the accused was charged, along with three others, with keeping a public gaming-house. The accused objected to the relevancy of the indictment on the basis that the crime charged was not one known to the law of Scotland. Lord Justice-Clerk Boyle said:

> "I have looked into the authorities on this subject, and I have found enough to satisfy my mind, that there are solid principles in our law

to justify a charge of this nature. It is of no consequence that the charge is now made for the first time."

He went on to refer to Hume and the power of the High Court to punish every act which is obviously of a criminal nature: "This court has a power to declare anything that has a tendency to corrupt public morals, and injure the interests of society, an indictable offence." The plea to relevancy was refused. Lord Cockburn dissented in this case and his view, that the Court's power was not to declare new crimes but to declare an existing crime, committed in a new way, has been very influential.

There continues to be debate and conflicting opinion over whether the power has been used this century. Many have argued that there are cases where the Court has declared a new crime and that this is a *de facto* use of the declaratory power. Other commentators have viewed these cases as examples of an existing principle being applied to a new set of facts. The cases in this group generally involve a plea to the relevancy of the indictment or the complaint on the basis that no such crime exists and include: *Strathern v. Seaforth* (1926) where it was held that "joyriding" amounts to the crime of clandestine use; *Kerr v. Hill* (1936) where the court held that it was a crime to give false information to the police; *Watt v. Annan* (1978) where organising the showing of a pornographic film in a private club was held to amount to shameless indecency; *Khaliq v. H.M. Advocate* (1984) where the supply of glue-sniffing kits was held to amount to causing real injury; *H.M. Advocate v. Wilson* (1984) where shutting off the electricity grid by pressing an emergency-stop button, resulting in economic loss rather than physical damage, was held to amount to malicious mischief; *S v. H.M. Advocate* (1989) which established that a husband could be prosecuted for the rape of his wife with whom he was still cohabiting at the time of the alleged offence; and *Normand v. Morrison* (1993) where it was held that letting police search a bag containing a contaminated needle amounted to reckless injury.

While there are no twentieth or twenty-first century cases where the power has been explicitly used, there are cases where the Court has refused to create a new crime. In *Grant v. Allan* (1987) the Appeal Court held that the clandestine taking of computer lists of customer information was not an offence known to Scottish law and the complaint was dismissed. Lord Justice-Clerk Ross and Lord McDonald acknowledged that to do otherwise would be creating a new crime and that this was the proper remit of Parliament.

The main objection to the declaratory power is based upon the principle of legality enshrined in Scots law. This principle expressed in the Latin maxim, *nullem crimen sine lege*, is that no one should be punished for an act that was not legally proscribed at the time of commission. The principle also probably requires that each crime should be capable of fairly precise definition so that its application to any particular set of facts can be clearly seen. Contravention of the principle of legality is also contravention of Article 7(1) of the Convention, which states that:

"No-one shall be held guilty of any criminal offence on account of an act or omission which did not constitute a criminal offence under national or international law at the time it was committed."

READING

C. Gane, C. Stoddart and J. Chalmers, *A Casebook on Scottish Criminal Law* (3rd ed., W. Green & Son, Edinburgh, 2001), Chap. 1.

G. H. Gordon, *Criminal Law* (3rd ed., M. Christie (ed.), W. Green & Son, Edinburgh, 2000), Vol. I, Chaps 1 and 2.

T. Jones and M. Christie, *Criminal Law* (2nd ed., W. Green & Son, Edinburgh, 1996), Vol. I, Chaps 1 and 2.

R. McCall Smith and D. Sheldon, *Scots Criminal Law* (Butterworths, Edinburgh, 1997), Chap. 1.

---

2. CRIMINAL RESPONSIBILITY

The definition of each common law crime is made up of a mental element (*mens rea*) and a physical element (*actus reus*). To understand both the content of substantive criminal law and also what is required to be proven for criminal responsibility to be established, both elements of each crime must be known. By approaching criminal law in this way, the student will grasp both the essential elements of criminal law and will appreciate the complexity and depth of the subject. It should be noted that all statutory crimes comprise a physical element, an *actus reus*, and some, but not all, have a mental element, a *mens rea*. Those crimes which do not have a requirement for a mental element are referred to as strict liability offences and are examined in this Chapter.

In addition to proving that the requisite *mens rea* and *actus reus* of a crime are present, it must also be shown that they coincide in time and that there is a causative link between the actions of the accused and the harm caused. These are the essential elements of criminal responsibility.

MENS REA

The basis of criminal responsibility is expressed in the Latin maxim, *actus non facit reum nisi mens sit rea* which means—roughly translated—that the act cannot be guilty unless the mind is also guilty. *Mens rea* literally means guilty mind.

One of the basic principles of legal and criminal responsibility is that those who are punished are those who deserve it, *i.e.* those who are considered to be morally or individually as well as factually responsible for what has been done. This is why the proof of the *mens rea*, or mental element, of any crime is important as it will reveal whether the accused has committed the crime with the requisite mental element to be found criminally liable rather than having merely acted accidentally without the requisite mental state.

Before examining the different types of *mens rea* it is worth noting that the term *mens rea* is a relatively new one in Scots law which has been imported from English law. The term that preceded it, which also referred to the mental element of any crime, was "dole". Dole is derived from the Latin *dolus* which is translated as "evil". Dole was defined by Hume as "that corrupt and evil intention, which is essential ... to the guilt of any crime" (i, 21). The emphasis on evil, immorality and bad character are reflective of the historical period when this was written. As attitudes to criminal behaviour and offenders have changed over time, such moral condemnation for the character of the modern criminal are perhaps now restricted to the most serious crimes, *e.g.* murder and assault. The modern use and understanding of *mens rea*, as the mental element in crime, has become dominant in both common law and statutory crimes. Be aware, however, that continued reference to terms such as "wicked recklessness" in the crime of murder and "evil intention" in the crime of assault, indicate that the modern law has not yet completely abandoned history.

Proving *Mens Rea*
It is necessary to establish whether the test for *mens rea* is objective or subjective. A subjective approach to *mens rea* requires that the accused had actually foreseen the consequences of his actions whereas if the objective approach is adopted the accused will be judged by the standards of the reasonable person. The reasonable person test is merely an objective prediction of how the reasonable person would have behaved in the circumstances, and the accused's behaviour is compared to this. An objective test is applied in Scots law (*Blane v. H.M. Advocate* (1991)).

The use of an objective test allows the prosecution to prove the *mens rea* by inference from the evidence led, *i.e.* the actions of the accused and the other surrounding circumstances. In the case *Cawthorne v. H.M. Advocate* (1968) Lord Justice Asquith stated at (p. 33):

"It is impossible ... to look into the mind of the man, and when, therefore, you are seeking to evaluate the effect of the evidence in regard to the nature and purposes of the act you can only do so by drawing an inference from what that man did in the background of all the facts of the case which you accept as proved."

Note that *mens rea* and motive are not the same thing. Motive is concerned with the reason why an individual acted as she did. Although the motive of the accused may be important in terms of the evidence which is led at her trial and the punishment given, it is not considered when determining whether or not she is criminally responsible, *e.g.* to kill someone deliberately out of a humanitarian motive would still be murder.

Categories of *Mens Rea*

The most commonly used categories or types of *mens rea* in both common law and statutory crimes are intention, recklessness and knowledge. Most crimes will only have one form of *mens rea* but there are exceptions that have more than one, *e.g.* murder. There are, however, other degrees of *mens rea* that will not be examined here, including, *e.g.* wilfulness and shamelessness.

Intention

Intention suggests deliberate action and can be found in the definition of many crimes including murder (intent to kill), theft (intent to deprive), assault (evil intent) and fraud (fraudulent intent). While intending an action is a subjective state of mind, proving that state of mind involves an objective test, as noted above. This is perhaps best illustrated by example. In the case of assault, the intention of the accused can be inferred from the action of punching another. It is not necessary to prove that the accused intended the consequence of his actions, *e.g.* a broken nose, merely that the punch was deliberate. Similarly, theft requires that an accused intended to deprive another person of their property. If, therefore, the accused removes a black jacket from a cloakroom in the belief that it is her own jacket, she cannot be said to have the necessary intention for the crime of theft.

The distinction between the *mens rea* of intention and recklessness has been blurred by references to a high degree of recklessness being equivalent to intention. In *Blane v. H.M. Advocate* (1991) Lord Justice-General Hope commented (at p. 581F) that:

"[S]ince the matter must be approached objectively I think it is open to inference, where the accused is shown to have acted with a reckless disregard for the likely consequences of what he does, that he intended those consequences to occur."

Blane approved the direction to the jury in *H.M. Advocate v. Boyd* (1977). In *Boyd,* Lord Kincraig directed the jury that the necessary intention to set fire to the subjects could be implied from conduct indicating an utter disregard of the likelihood of the fire spreading to the subjects in question. In both cases, therefore, a high degree of recklessness was treated as being equivalent to intention. *Byrne v. H.M. Advocate* (2000) overruled these earlier decisions. In *Byrne* (which involved a charge of wilful fire-raising), Lord Coulsfield notes (at p. 91C) that the confusion in *Boyd* may have arisen from Lord Kincraig having in mind the crime of murder, which can be committed both intentionally and with wicked recklessness. Wilful fire-raising, however, only has one *mens rea,* namely intention. *Byrne* overruled *Blane* in so far as it approved the direction to the jury in *H.M. Advocate v. Boyd* (1977). *Byrne* clarifies that in those crimes, where the *mens rea* is intention, a form of reckless *mens rea*, regardless of the degree, will not be adequate for intention to be inferred.

Transferred Intention
Problems arise where the anticipated result of an accused's actions is affected by external circumstances. Examples include where A throws a bottle intending to hit B and, as a result of being a poor aim, misses and hits C. The question which arises in these circumstances is can A be charged with assault when he intended to hit B but missed and hit C? The *actus reus* of assault is fulfilled but can the *mens rea* be transferred? Case law suggests that the *mens rea* can be transferred and this is described as "transferred intention". One case that illustrates transferred intent is *Roberts v. Hamilton* (1989). Roberts was convicted at the sheriff court of assaulting Crawford and appealed to the High Court on the grounds that she lacked the requisite *mens rea*. The facts of the case were that Roberts had attempted to separate her cohabitee and her son who were fighting with each other. She intended to strike her cohabitee with a stick but missed and instead struck Crawford. The High Court refused the appeal.

In *Roberts v. Hamilton* the High Court confirmed the view of Hume that criminal responsibility will arise where the accused has assaulted A in the belief that she is B, or alternatively, A in error when she aimed at B (Hume, i, 22). This approach has been overruled to the extent that in more recent cases including *H.M. Advocate v. Harris* (1993) and *Byrne v. H.M. Advocate* (2000) the Court has expressed a different view of the law. In *Byrne* a bench of five judges rejected the application of the doctrine of transferred intent in cases of wilful fire-raising. Like assault, this crime can only be committed intentionally. In *Byrne,* the Court held (at p. 92) that:

"the jury may infer the necessary intention from all the relevant circumstances, but there is no room for the doctrine of transferred intent. Nor can any form of recklessness be treated as equivalent to intent ... before an accused can be convicted of wilful fire-raising in respect of any particular item of property in the charge, the Crown must establish that he intended to set fire to that item of property."

The judgment of the Court did not refer to *Roberts v. Hamilton,* however, if such an approach was adopted, it would appear that a charge of assault could not succeed and conviction would only follow if an alternative charge of reckless injury had been libelled.

Recklessness
Criminal recklessness was defined as "a total indifference to and disregard for the safety of the public" in *RHW v. H.M. Advocate* (1982, p. 420). Recklessness is determined by an objective test and does not require that the accused was aware of, or considered the possible risks from his behaviour (which would amount to a subjective test being applied, see *Allan v. Patterson* (1980)). Reliance on the subjective test

used in *Allan v. Patterson* (1980) has subsequently been described as "problematic" in *Carr v. H.M. Advocate* (1995), *Thomson v. H.M. Advocate* (1995) and *Cameron v. Maguire* (1999), which have reinforced that an objective test should be employed. An objective test results in the actions of the accused being considered against those of the "reasonable person" and the question is whether those actions demonstrate a complete or utter disregard of the consequences of the act in question. The use of such an objective test underlines that an accused is assumed to have some awareness of risk when carrying out a criminal or legal act. In homicide two forms of recklessness are recognised. In the crime of murder the *mens rea* includes wicked recklessness and in culpable homicide the *mens rea* is recklessness. These are examined in more depth in Chapter 3. [Please also see Appendix 2: Addendum on p. 99.]

Knowledge
The *mens rea* of knowledge is required in some crimes, *e.g.* in reset or in the crime of assaulting a police officer. In both instances the accused must know or reasonably suspect the status of either the goods in question or the individual. Evidence of actual conscious knowledge on the part of the accused may not be necessary if the evidence suggests that the accused ignored the obvious. In the case of *Latta v. Herron* (1967) the accused appealed against conviction of the reset of two guns. The sheriff at first instance had accepted that the accused was not conscious that the guns he had purchased were stolen but said that the full circumstances of whom they were purchased from and where this took place, etc., raised an inescapable inference that they were dishonestly obtained and the accused had "wilfully blinded himself to the obvious". The Appeal Court confirmed the finding of the sheriff and the appeal was dismissed.

Negligence
Negligence involves risk-taking or lack of care of a degree greater than would be expected of the "reasonable person". While this is similar to recklessness, they are differentiated by the degree of risk-taking or carelessness. The common law does not regard merely negligent behaviour as criminal. In some statutory offences, however, negligence would be adequate *mens rea* to constitute criminal liability, *e.g.* careless driving.

Error and Absence of *Mens Rea*
Error is relevant in two contexts. First, where the accused, as a result of the error, lacks the necessary *mens rea* for the crime charged. Secondly, error can also result in the accused believing that his intentional actions were justifiable.

Absence of Mens Rea

The first category of error is where, as a result of error, the accused lacks the necessary *mens rea* for the crime charged. In these circumstances, she cannot be held responsible for the crime. This scenario would arise where, *e.g.* an accused takes a shopping bag in the belief that it is her own, therefore lacking the intention to deprive another of their property (which would be necessary in the crime of theft). However, such errors of judgement do not always serve to negate criminal responsibility, namely, where the error is reckless. In such a scenario, although the accused may lack the necessary intention to commit a crime, her reckless mental state may fulfil the *mens rea* requirement of certain crimes. This is illustrated in respect of the crime of rape where it has been held that if an accused has recklessly formed a belief that the woman is consenting to intercourse and she is not, this reckless error will not serve as a defence (*Jamieson v. H.M. Advocate* (1994)).

An error occurring in the commission of a crime will not serve to negate criminal responsibility, however, if the essential ingredients of *mens rea* and *actus reus* are still present. For example, in the case of *Andrew Ewart* (1828) the accused and his victim were guarding a graveyard. The accused mistook his companion for a body snatcher and shot and killed him. He was charged and convicted of murder, since it would in fact have been murder if he had killed an actual body snatcher.

Intentional Actions and Error

The second category of error is relevant when the accused acts intentionally but in the belief that these actions are justifiable. Here the nature of the error is significant in relation to whether or not it will be deemed to be acceptable in law. There are two types of error in this group: (a) errors of law and (b) errors of fact. Errors, which arise through mere ignorance of the law, are not recognised. As a matter of public policy people are presumed to know the law. Factual errors may be recognised if they fulfil certain criteria.

(a) Error of Law. In *Clark v. Syme* (1957) the respondent was charged with maliciously shooting and killing a neighbour's sheep. His defence was that he thought his actions were legal because he had forewarned his neighbour that sheep were damaging his crops and that he would shoot any animals that wandered onto his land. His defence of error of law was accepted at trial and he was acquitted. The prosecutor appealed by way of stated case to the High Court. Lord Justice-General Clyde said (at p. 5): "the mere fact that his criminal act was performed under a misconception of what legal remedies he might otherwise have had, does not make it any less criminal".

On some occasions an error of law can serve to negate the *mens rea* of a crime. This would apply where an accused takes property in the erroneous belief that it belongs to her. In these circumstances, the accused will lack the intention to deprive the owner of their property which is the *mens rea* of theft. This is called an erroneous claim of right and can act as a defence to a charge of theft. Such a defence is not available where an accused takes property, never believing it to belong to her, but in the belief that it is not criminal to do so. The question of erroneous claim of right was raised in *Dewar v. H.M. Advocate* (1945).

In *Dewar* the appellant, a crematorium manager, had been convicted of the theft of two coffins and a number of coffin lids. He appealed against conviction and sentence. At trial his defence was that he mistakenly believed that following their delivery to him he was entitled to dispose of the coffins and coffin lids as he wished, and that this was the common practice at other crematoria. During his evidence Dewar conceded that his belief as to the practice at other crematoria was wrong and there was insufficient evidence to support his belief. Lord Justice-General Normand said (at pp. 11–12):

"[T]he presiding judge took a lenient view when he instructed the jury to consider whether the appellant might have entertained an honest and reasonable belief, based on colourable grounds, that he was entitled to treat the coffins as 'scrap'. The presiding judge pointed out that the jury must not exculpate the appellant merely because he entertained an erroneous belief founded on some singular notions of his own, but that they must discover some evidence that he had rational and colourable grounds for believing that he was entitled to remove, retain and dispose of the coffin lids."

The Appeal Court refused the appeal, finding that the direction by the trial judge was not only fair but lenient to the accused. Lord Justice-General Normand indicated that the defence of error was irrelevant in *Dewar* as there was adequate evidence upon which the jury were able to convict of theft.

(b) Error of Fact. An error of fact can serve to justify an accused's actions if it is both honest and reasonable. In *Owens v. H.M. Advocate* (1946) the accused believed his attacker had a knife and was about to kill him and so he killed the attacker in self-defence. He was convicted and on appeal the conviction was quashed due to the fact that the jury had been misdirected at the trial on the question of self-defence. The opinion of the Court was that if the jury had come to the conclusion that the appellant genuinely believed that he was gravely threatened by a man armed with a knife but the deceased actually had no knife in his hand, it would have been their duty to acquit, and the jury ought to have been so directed. This case suggests that the actions of an accused must be both honest and reasonable if an error of fact is to serve to justify the accused's actions.

The requirement that a factual error be both honest and reasonable is accepted as now applying to all crimes except that of rape following *Meek v. H.M. Advocate* (1983) and *Jamieson v. H.M. Advocate* (1994). In *Meek* a number of men were convicted of rape. The Appeal Court noted that the evidence presented at the trial was of two conflicting accounts of the incident. The complainer gave evidence that she had not consented to intercourse whilst the evidence of the accused was that she had consented. The defence of error was not pled, however, Lord Justice Emslie stated (at p. 281):

"[W]e have no difficulty in accepting that an essential element in the crime of rape is the absence of an honest belief that the woman is consenting. The criminal intent is, after all, to force intercourse upon a woman against her will ... The absence of reasonable grounds for such an alleged belief will, however, have a considerable bearing upon whether any jury will accept that such an 'honest belief' was held."

The Court accepted that the proper test is whether a belief is honest and the reasonableness of that belief in consent is only relevant in relation to the credibility of the accused. In *Meek* the Court adopted the law as had been laid down in *R. v. Morgan* (1976) that an honest belief, even if it is held on unreasonable grounds, is sufficient to negate the necessary intention required for the crime of rape and therefore the accused should be acquitted. The Court did not consider whether this departure from the traditional "honest and reasonable" test applied to other areas of law.

The Court's opinion in *Meek* on this point was *obiter dictum* (an opinion on a point that is not essential to the decision), however, it was regarded as authority for the departure from the rule that any error required to be both honest and reasonable. This was subsequently confirmed in *Jamieson v. H.M. Advocate* (1994) where the accused appealed against conviction of rape on the grounds that the jury had been misdirected that his belief that the woman was consenting to intercourse required to be both honest and reasonable. At trial he had admitted having intercourse with the complainer and that she had, at the time, resisted but that he thought she wished to have intercourse. The accused in this case was, therefore, claiming that his error as to the woman's consent negated the *mens rea* of intention, necessary for the crime of rape. The appeal was successful and the conviction was quashed. Lord Justice-General Hope delivering the opinion of the Court stated (at p. 186A–C):

"The crime of rape consists in the carnal knowledge of a woman forcibly and against her will. Thus, the *mens rea* of this crime includes the intention to have intercourse with the woman without her consent. The absence of the belief that she was consenting is an essential element in it. If a man has intercourse with a woman in the belief that she is consenting to this, he cannot be guilty of rape. Now, the question whether the man believed that the woman consented is a question of fact. It is a question that the jury must decide, if it is raised, on the evidence. The grounds for his belief will be important and if he has reasonable grounds for it, the jury may find it easier to accept that he did honestly believe that the woman consented. But it will be open to the jury to accept his evidence on this point even if he cannot give grounds for it that they consider to be reasonable, and if they accept his evidence they must acquit him. This is because the question is whether he genuinely or honestly believed that the woman was consenting to intercourse. It will not do if he acted without thinking or was indifferent as to whether or not he had her consent. The man must have genuinely formed the belief that she was consenting to his having intercourse with her. But this need not be a belief which the jury regards as reasonable, so long as they are satisfied that his belief was genuinely held by him at the time."

Jamieson clarifies that in the crime of rape the *mens rea* can be either intention or recklessness ("it will not do if he acted without thinking or was indifferent as to whether or not he had her consent" (p. 186B)) and that the accused's belief in the complainer's consent only requires to be honest and not reasonable if it is to lead to acquittal.

The Court in *Jamieson* made it clear that this change in the approach to error will only apply to rape and not other instances, *e.g.* in the case of self-defence. Lord Justice-General Hope stated that the reason why a man's belief need not be reasonable in rape cases is because of the particular nature of the *mens rea* required to commit the crime (pp. 186G–187A). Both Gordon in his commentary on this case (pp. 188 and 189) and Christie (2000, p. 415) note that it is difficult to see how other cases are easily differentiated from rape in respect of error requiring to be both honest and reasonable.

ACTUS REUS

The term *actus reus* has no official or accepted meaning but is generally used to denote the physical element of crime that the law wishes to prevent. *Actus reus* includes the conduct, omission or situation which, if accompanied by an appropriate state of mind, would result in criminal responsibility. Criminal responsibility, for the most part, depends on the performance of overt acts. A criminal or anti-social thought is not enough to lead to a conviction.

In conduct crimes, the *actus reus* is the "conduct" required, *e.g.* in assault it is "any attack upon the person of another which causes fear or alarm". In "result crimes", the *actus reus* is the conduct which brings about the result, *e.g.* in murder, the *actus reus* is "a wilful act causing the destruction of human life". The law does not classify different methods of taking life as different *actus reus*. Rather, it is the taking of life rather than the mode of doing so that is relevant.

It is necessary that the accused voluntarily brought about the wrong that has occurred. In most cases this requirement is easily fulfilled. However, there are occasions when the accused is not deemed to have acted voluntarily either because of things which occur that are outwith her control or where she has had a lack of control over her own actions. Where an accused has carried out a criminal act, without this essential self-control, then no criminal responsibility will attach. Examples of this can be seen in cases where the harm caused is as a result of bad weather as in *Hogg v. Macpherson* (1928) or where the accused has acted as an automaton because of external, non self-induced factors as in *Ross v. H.M. Advocate* (1991). Automatism is fully considered in Chapter 6.

There is no definitive list of the *actus reus* of common law crimes. Rather, each crime has a particular *actus reus*. Whereas statutory offences narrate the relevant *actus reus* in the section of the statute, the *actus reus* of common law crimes is found by consulting the works of the institutional writers and court opinions. Both common law and statutory offences sometimes require a number of different types of conduct for the *actus reus*. For example, the common law crime of uttering as genuine, requires both a forged document and the presentation of it as genuine to another person. In *George Skene Edwards* (1827) a jury returned a verdict of guilty of forgery alone on a charge of "uttering as genuine". The conviction was quashed on appeal as "forgery" did not amount to a known crime. If an accused person has completed some of the essential steps towards fulfilment of the *actus reus* of a crime, she may, however, be convicted of an attempt to commit that crime.

Although there is not a definitive list of the *actus reus* used in common law crimes it is useful to classify *actus reus* into three groups:

(1) an overt or positive act;
(2) an omission; and
(3) state of affairs.

(1) An Overt or Positive Act

It is generally assumed that all actions are overt or positive. Whilst such actions may involve a physical movement of the body, an overt or positive act can also refer to types of conduct, *e.g.* in the crime of breach of the peace, "conducting yourself in a disorderly manner and committing a breach of the peace". As noted above, such an overt or positive act is assumed to be voluntary. Actions that are shown to have been induced by an external factor, over which the accused has no control, will generally not be regarded as criminal.

(2) An Omission

Omissions do not generally attract criminal responsibility in Scots common law. In a small number of statutes criminal responsibility will arise where the accused fails to do something. For example, section 172 of the Road Traffic Act 1988 requires the owner or keeper of a vehicle to give information to the police as to the identity of the driver of that vehicle at a material time. This requirement was held not to be a breach of the Convention in *Jardine v. Crowe* (1999).

In respect of the common law, there is no assumption of the Good Samaritan and, therefore, an individual who finds another in peril is not legally obliged to intervene and assist that person. There are certain situations, however, where such intervention is legally required and failure to intervene will result in criminal liability. This includes:

(a) where a dangerous situation has been created by the accused or where the prior actions of the accused has created danger;
(b) where the accused's status or contractual obligations result in a duty to act; and
(c) where there is a prior relationship between the accused and the victim which is such that there is a legal obligation to act.

(a) Where the accused has created a dangerous situation. In this type of situation the accused's omission generally follows a prior positive act. The prior positive act may be non-criminal as in *McPhail v. Clark* (1983) where a fire deliberately set to burn straw spread to the adjacent roadside and the resultant smoke created a dangerous situation for motorists and a number of vehicles crashed. The farmer was convicted of recklessly endangering the lieges. His action of allowing the fire to spread and doing nothing about it for at least 20 minutes, when it was assumed he must have seen what was happening, was held by the sheriff to demonstrate a reckless indifference to the consequences for the public generally and for the particular road users directly affected by his actions.

There are occasions where the prior actions of the accused are themselves criminal. In *H.M. Advocate v. McPhee* (1935) the accused was charged with murder. The indictment alleged that he had assaulted a woman, compressed her throat with his hands, beat her with his fists, knocked her to the ground and kicked her repeatedly, and "did expose her in the said field while in an injured and unconscious condition to the inclemency of the weather". The accused lodged a preliminary plea to the relevancy of the charge that was repelled by the court. Lord Mackay stated (at p. 50) that there could be a murder conviction if it was proved that the accused "wickedly and feloniously exposed the unconscious woman regardless of consequences to the inclemency of the weather, and if she died in consequence ... both of the beating and the exposure." At trial, the accused was convicted of culpable homicide.

In cases of this sort, if it can be proven that the accused's initial criminal actions caused the victim's death, then the question of omission will not arise. However, where the accused's initial criminal action has weakened the condition of the victim, then the accused has a responsibility to either remove the victim or obtain help to aid them in the dangerous situation she has created.

(b) Where the accused's status or contractual obligations result in a duty to act. This would apply to people in public office or a position of responsibility. Liability would arise in this situation where the individual had a duty to prevent the occurrence of harm and will be liable for any harm arising from her failure to discharge such a duty. In the case of *Bonar and Hogg v. MacLeod* (1983) the accused (a police officer) failed to intervene to prevent the assault of a person in police custody by an officer junior to himself. He was regarded as art and part liable for the said assault. In *William Hardie* (1847) Hardie was a Poor Law inspector who was convicted of culpable homicide when death resulted from his failure to deal with an application for assistance. Liability will arise where the accused fails to discharge the duties imposed by his position.

(c) Where there is a prior relationship between the accused and the victim which is such that there is a legal obligation to act. Although the idea of the Good Samaritan or "being your brother's keeper" is generally not embraced in Scots criminal law, it is assumed that a legal obligation to protect will exist in relationships between, *e.g.* a parent and a minor child. The only reported Scottish authorities, concern mothers who failed to summon help at the birth of children who subsequently died, *e.g. H.M. Advocate v. Scott* (1892).

This type of legal obligation would not, however, be assumed to pertain to all other relationships. If a relationship of dependence does arise, however, a legal obligation to protect may follow, *e.g.* an obligation to protect could arise where a householder has a long-term lodger who is gravely ill. Failure to summon medical assistance in these circumstances may result in criminal responsibility. In the English case *R. v. Instan* (1893) the accused lived with her aged aunt whom she neglected by not giving her any food for 10 days and failed to obtain medical help to deal with the gangrene her aunt had developed. As a result, the aunt died and the accused was convicted of manslaughter. Both the family relationship and, more importantly, the relationship of dependence between the two parties resulted in the niece having a legal obligation to protect. While there is no reported case law on this specific point in Scotland it is assumed that *Instan* would be followed.

Is there a Duty to Prevent the Commission of a Crime?
There is no Scottish authority to the effect that a person who fails to take steps to prevent a crime does thereby commit an offence. In *H.M. Advocate v. Kerr* (1871) one of the three men accused of assault with intent to ravish had not participated in the assault but had watched from the adjoining field. The jury were directed that they should not convict the accused in the absence of evidence that he had encouraged the others by language or presence. Presence, at the scene of a crime may result in criminal responsibility and this will be discussed below in more detail in the context of art and part liability.

(3) State of Affairs
The third type of *actus reus* is state of affairs. This will normally be found in statutory offences, *e.g.* section 4(2) of the Road Traffic Act 1988 provides that a person who, when in charge of a mechanically propelled vehicle which is on a road or other public place, is unfit to drive through drink or drugs, is guilty of an offence. However, it does also appear in the common law crime of breach of the peace. In

Montgomery v. McLeod (1977) the accused was "found" by the police and was arrested by them when he refused to move on. At his appeal against conviction of breach of the peace Lord Justice-General Emslie stated (p. 165): "There is no limit to the kind of conduct which may give rise to a charge of breach of the peace."

CONCURRENCE OF *ACTUS REUS* AND *MENS REA*

The *actus reus* and *mens rea* must coincide in time if criminal liability is to be proved by the prosecution. Generally, the *mens rea* would be expected to proceed or occur contemporaneously with the *actus reus*. In *Thabo v. R.* (1954) the appellants were convicted of the murder of a man, whom they had assaulted and, believing that he was dead, thrown his body off a cliff. Medical evidence showed that the man had not been dead but that he did later die from exposure. The attempt by the appellants to argue that the *mens rea* and *actus reus* did not coincide in time was unsuccessful and the court held that they could not divide up what was a series of acts.

STRICT LIABILITY OFFENCES

Strict liability offences occur where there is no need to prove a mental element. Although this type of liability is only found in statutory offences, most statutory offences will conform to the usual rule that *mens rea* must be proven before there will be a conviction, *e.g. Sweet v. Parsley* (1970). In English law it is presumed that *mens rea* is required and it is for the prosecution to prove otherwise. While this may not be as clear cut in Scots criminal law, the common reliance on English precedent when interpreting statutes may result in the same approach ultimately being adopted in Scotland.

VICARIOUS LIABILITY

Vicarious liability occurs where one individual is held responsible for the actions of another. Vicarious liability is not recognised in respect of common law crimes and is presumed not to exist in relation to statutory crimes. It may be found in some statutes, *e.g.* where an employer may be held vicariously liable for their employee's acts. Vicarious liability offences are found in the Licensing Scotland Act 1976, s.67(2), where the licence holder may be held liable for the actions of an employee or agent.

CORPORATE LIABILITY

The prosecution of companies for strict liability offences is unproblematic. If *mens rea* is required to be proven, however, prosecution and conviction for certain crimes will be more difficult. In *Dean v. John Menzies Ltd* (1981) it was held that a company was not capable of forming the required *mens rea* for the crime of shameless indecency. Whilst it may be assumed that similar difficulties would be encountered in proving a charge of murder or culpable homicide, it should be noted that the Crown Office announced on February 28, 2002 that they are to indict the company Transco on a charge of culpable homicide. In crimes involving dishonesty it may be possible to prove the requisite *mens rea*, *e.g. Purcell Meats Ltd v. McLeod* (1987) where it was confirmed on appeal that a company could be guilty of fraud.

CAUSATION

Criminal responsibility requires proof of the *mens rea*, the *actus reus* and causation. Causation requires that the actions of the accused caused the harm suffered. In many cases causation is straightforward, *e.g.* in an assault where the accused has punched the victim on her nose, it is obvious that the accused has caused the harm suffered. The situation becomes more complicated, however, where an accused has carried out a wrongful act, *e.g.* a serious assault and thereafter complications with medical treatment occur and the victim dies. The question that then arises is whether it was the original assault or the medical treatment that caused the death.

While causation requires to be established for every crime, it tends to be more problematic in respect of the crimes of murder and culpable homicide. The importance of demonstrating the accused's responsibility for a death where there are intervening or pre-existing factors is obvious. In testing whether the necessary causative link exists, the characteristics of the victim, the conduct of the victim, the intervention of third parties (*e.g.* medical treatment) and the reasonable foreseeability of the outcome will be considered. These are guiding legal principles rather than strict legal rules. These guiding principles are examined below.

Characteristics of the Victim

This is also known as "taking your victim as you find him" or "the thin skull rule". This principle is commonly considered in the situation where a victim with a pre-existing medical condition is attacked and death results. The general approach adopted by the courts has been that the accused must take responsibility for his actions even where the victim has a pre-existing medical condition.

In *H.M. Advocate v. Robertson and Donoghue* (1945) the accused were charged with assault, robbery and murder. The case against the first accused was that he had assaulted an elderly shopkeeper, struggled with him and inflicted certain slight injuries on him. Medical evidence disclosed that the deceased had a very weak heart and that the elderly man died of heart failure. Robertson was found guilty of culpable homicide and the case against Donoghue was not proven. In his summing up, Lord Justice-Clerk Cooper said: "[I]t is none the less homicide to accelerate or precipitate the death of an ailing person than it is to cut down a healthy man who might have lived for fifty years."

The characteristics of the deceased have also been recognised as including, *e.g.* religious beliefs, as is illustrated by the English case *R. v. Blaue* (1975). The accused was charged with the murder of a young woman by stabbing her. The woman had been taken to hospital where she had refused a blood transfusion because she was a Jehovah's Witness. She did not receive a transfusion and died four hours later. It was accepted that she would have survived if she had accepted the transfusion. The accused was convicted of manslaughter on the basis of diminished responsibility and appealed against conviction. The appeal was dismissed and Lord Justice Lawton said (at p.450):

"The physical cause of death in this case was the bleeding into the pleural cavity arising from the penetration of the lung. This had not been brought about by any decision made by the deceased girl but by the stab wound."

This case is persuasive authority that both the physical and psychological characteristics of the victim must be taken as found by the perpetrator.

Conduct of the Victim
Even in situations where the voluntary actions of the victim have contributed to the harm suffered, this has not served to break the chain of causation. Examples of this are found where an accused is held responsible for supplying noxious substances that the victim voluntarily ingests, where the victim does not mitigate the effects of injuries inflicted and where the victim deliberately harms himself.

Noxious Substances
Recent cases have established that an accused who supplies noxious substances will be held responsible for any harm resulting from their voluntary ingestion by the victim. This relates to substances that are themselves legal and illegal.

In *Khaliq v. H.M. Advocate* (1984) two shopkeepers who sold glue-sniffing kits to children were charged with causing real injury. The Court held that the voluntary acts of the children after they purchased the kits did not constitute a *novus actus interveniens*. Lord Justice-General Emslie (at p. 144) said:

"Where, as in the case of charge (1), there is no intervention of third party action, or of an unexpected event entirely external to the transaction between the parties directly concerned, there appears to be no ground upon which it can be successfully maintained, upon the basis of *novus actus interveniens*, that the inhalation of the noxious fumes of the solvents by the voluntary and deliberate acts of the recipients of the supply, is fatal to the relevancy of such a charge as is exemplified by charge (1) in this indictment."

The Court said the actions of the recipients were entirely expected and were the known specific purpose of the supply. The accused pled guilty as charged.

The criminal responsibility of those who supply illegal drugs for ingestion by others was confirmed in *Lord Advocate's Reference (No. 1 of 1994)* (1995). The Court confirmed the approach adopted in the earlier cases of *Khaliq* and *Ulhaq v. H.M. Advocate* (1991) namely, that the chain of causation is not broken merely because a voluntary act by the recipient of the drugs is required to produce the injuries, harm or death that occurs.

Victims and Mitigation of Harm
Victims are generally not assumed to be responsible for mitigating the harm they have suffered. This can arise in a number of contexts, including where the victim is fatally injured when trying to escape an attack. Case law suggests that in these circumstances the accused will be held responsible for the death of the victim. In *Patrick Slaven* (1885) a woman was attacked by the accused who intended to rape her. When she attempted to escape the accused pursued her and she fell over a cliff and died. The accused's conduct was held to be the cause of the woman's death.

The question of mitigation of harm may also arise where the victim of an assault does not follow medical advice and subsequently dies. In the case *Jos. and Mary Norris* (1886) the two accused were charged with the culpable homicide of a man whom they had assaulted. None of the wounds inflicted had been serious and the victim received prompt medical treatment. However, the man had died eight days later from tetanus. There was evidence that the man had ignored medical advice, drunk alcohol and removed his own bandages. Lord Craighill directed the jury that if they believed the tetanus was brought on by the deceased's actions rather than the attack then the accused were entitled to be acquitted. But if their belief was that the tetanus had been caused by the attack and would have developed regardless of how the accused had behaved then the verdict would have to be one of guilty. The jury returned a verdict of "not proven". The direction to the jury in this case has been regarded as somewhat unusual and it is generally assumed that an accused will be responsible for the consequences of their actions regardless of how the victim has behaved. In a case such as that above, however, where the original injuries are minor the duties on an accused may not be as onerous.

Victims who Deliberately Harm Themselves
If the victim of an assault deliberately self harms and accelerates her death, the perpetrator of the original assault may still be held responsible for her death. This would be dependent upon whether the actions of the accused were deemed to be a cause of death. There is no Scots case law on this point, however, in the U.S. case *People v. Lewis* (1899) the accused shot his victim in the stomach and then put him to bed. A few minutes later the victim cut his throat. Medical evidence suggested that the gun-shot wound would have caused death within one hour and the

cut throat would have caused death within five minutes. The accused was convicted of manslaughter and unsuccessfully appealed. His actions were deemed to have contributed to the victim's death and the throat cutting did not serve to break the chain of causation.

Intervening Causes
Proof of causation becomes more complex where there are intervening events between the actions of the accused and the death of the victim. It is unusual for an intervening event to break the chain of causation unless it is truly independent of the harm caused by the accused. An intervening event which does break the chain of causation is known as a *novus actus interveniens*. Case law demonstrates that courts are reluctant to recognise intervening causes as breaking the chain of causation. The effects of intervening causes will be examined under three headings: assault and subsequent infection; inadequate medical treatment; and, other medical intervention.

Assault and Subsequent Infection
In general, the law will not recognise external intervening causes as breaking the chain of causation unless they prove to be a wholly unpredictable cause of death. Therefore, in those cases where a victim of a serious assault develops a wound infection and dies this would not break the chain of causation (see *James Wilson* (1838)). However, if the victim of a non-fatal assault were to contract an illness while in hospital and die as a result of that illness, this would most probably be seen to be a new and unpredictable cause of death unrelated to the actions of the accused. This is illustrated by the U.S. case *Bush v. Commonwealth* (1880) where the victim had suffered a gun-shot wound and thereafter died from scarlet fever while in hospital. It was held that his death was as a result of contracting the disease and not the original assault. Both this case and that of *James Wilson* (1838) emphasise that before a subsequent infection will be treated as a *novus actus interveniens* it must be independent of the original injury.

Inadequate Medical Treatment
Inadequate medical treatment is also known as malregimen. Where the injury or wound is serious, intervening poor medical treatment will not break the chain of causation and the perpetrator will be held responsible for the resulting death. However, if the wound or injury is so minor that without the poor medical treatment it would not have caused death, then the poor medical treatment will serve as a *novus actus interveniens* (*James Williamson* (1866)). The question is, therefore, one of foreseeability and whether it was foreseeable that the actions of the accused would cause the death of the victim.

Other Medical Intervention
The impact of other medical intervention would arise, *e.g.* where an assault victim's life-support machine is turned off. In *Finlayson v. H.M. Advocate* (1979) the victim had suffered brain death following the injection of a controlled drug. The High Court held that turning off the life-support machine was foreseeable and did not break the chain of causation. The effects of the injection were held to be the substantial and continuing cause of death.

ART AND PART LIABILITY

Art and part liability, sometimes referred to as acting in concert, arises where two or more individuals participate in the commission of a crime. This participation can be the result of a common plan or purpose, or can arise spontaneously. Whilst the criminal law will generally only hold an accused responsible for their individual actions, where a common purpose, *i.e.* art and part liability can be established, the accused will be held responsible for the actions of others within the group. This may appear unreasonable if an individual has only offered minor assistance, *e.g.* as a "lookout" in a bank robbery. Although the different levels of participation will not affect criminal responsibility they will, however, be taken into account at the point of sentencing. Conversely, if a number of people are involved in a criminal incident but no common purpose, either planned or spontaneous can be shown, then each will be judged only on the basis of their own actions. Art and part liability applies to both common law and statutory offences.

Participation and Degrees of Involvement
Art and part guilt can result from different types of participation in a criminal purpose. These include the provision of material assistance prior to the commission of the crime and physical assistance at the time of commission of the crime. Art and part liability will also apply to situations where an offence is committed at the instigation of someone else. Therefore where an assassin is hired, both the assassin and the hirer will be held art and part liable for any crime that is committed as part of the common plan.

Counsel or Instigation
Counsel or instigation refers to the situation where advice is given in respect of the commission of a crime or where the perpetrator's commission of a crime is instigated by others. In both scenarios, where there is a common plan, all parties involved will be held responsible for the commission of the crime. Where a group of individuals conspire to commit a crime, their agreement is adequate to attract art and part liability. General advice will not constitute either counsel or instigation (Hume, i, 278). Any counsel or instigation must be given before the crime is carried out. In *Martin v. Hamilton* (1989) a solicitor was charged with contravening section 176 of the Road Traffic Act 1972,

which makes it an offence to aid, abet, counsel, procure or incite another person to commit an offence against the provisions of that Act. The charge was held to be irrelevant as the client had failed to report a road traffic accident at the first opportunity and, therefore, had already committed the crime by the time he allegedly saw the solicitor and was advised not to report the accident.

Provision of Material Assistance
Prior to art and part guilt being established on the basis of material assistance, it must be shown that the parties have participated in a common plan to commit a crime. If this can be shown, the level of assistance provided is irrelevant in establishing criminal responsibility, however any assistance must have been provided prior to the commission of the crime. Although the provider of assistance need not be aware of every aspect of the crime planned or have participated in the commission of the crime, it is clear that they must be aware that they are assisting a criminal purpose. There must also be some connection between the actual perpetrator of the harm and the assistance provider.

In *H.M. Advocate v. Johnstone and Stewart* (1926) the two accused were charged with procuring an abortion while acting in concert. The two women had never met, however, Johnstone had obtained Stewart's name from a third party and had passed this onto persons interested in obtaining an abortion. Lord Moncrieff directed the jury that if they accepted the evidence that the women were strangers and that no money was paid by Stewart to Johnstone for the referral, then art and part guilt could not be established. Johnstone was acquitted and Stewart convicted.

Assistance at the Commission of the Crime

Common Plan. *H.M. Advocate v. Lappen* (1956) provides a good example of art and part guilt arising from a common plan. In this case, the accused and five others were charged with assault and robbery. Lord Patrick directed the jury (at p. 110):
> "[I]f a number of men form a common plan whereby some are to commit the actual seizure of the property, and some according to the plan are to keep watch, and some according to the plan are to help to carry away the loot, and some according to the plan are to help to dispose of the loot, then, although the actual robbery may only have been committed by one or two of them, every one is guilty of the robbery because they joined together in a common plan to commit the robbery."

Spontaneous Common Purpose. A spontaneous common purpose is most likely to be found in relation to crimes of violence. One would not expect, *e.g.* a group of people to spontaneously decide to rob a bank and obviously this type of crime is more likely to be planned or at least openly agreed to in advance. In *Gallacher v. H.M. Advocate* (1951) three accused were part of a larger group who stood around a man and kicked him to death. There was no evidence that this attack was planned or that there had been prior agreement. The spontaneous attack on the man was viewed as the common purpose and all three were convicted of murder.

Unforeseen Consequences
Lappen provides a relatively straightforward example of art and part guilt, however, this becomes more complex when things are done that are not part of the common plan. It must then be decided if all partners to the common plan are responsible for this unforeseen incident or whether the perpetrator should be held solely responsible. For example, if a group of individuals agree to rob a bank and have fake guns and one of the group produces a real gun and shoots the teller dead, should all of the group be held responsible for this death? When deciding this question the courts have focussed on whether the unplanned actions were reasonably foreseeable. If they are, all of the group will be held responsible.

The approach adopted in recent cases including *Boyne v. H.M. Advocate* (1980) and *Codona v. H.M. Advocate* (1996) indicate that the blanket responsibility that was once assumed to accompany evidence of a common plan in, *e.g. H.M. Advocate v. Gallacher* (1950) is now more fragile. Individual responsibility is now more closely examined and both the foresight, *mens rea* and participation of each accused is more carefully examined.

In *Boyne v. H.M. Advocate* (1980) three accused were charged and convicted of murder. The victim had been stabbed with a knife and there was evidence that this was not part of the common plan. The Lord Justice-Clerk found that there was nothing to show that the two appellants knew or had reasonable cause to believe that the actual killer would use a knife on the victim. There appears to have been evidence that one of them knew that the killer sometimes carried a knife, but it appears that he believed that it was for self-defence and had never seen him use the knife in previous assaults. As an alternative ground of responsibility, the judge considered that if either co-accused had carried on with the assault after they saw the knife being used this would have made them art and part guilty. The murder convictions of the two accused who did not have the knife were quashed and verdicts of guilty of robbery and assault substituted.

In *Codona* the appellant, a fourteen-year-old girl, had been convicted art and part of murder and appealed to the High Court on the ground that there was insufficient evidence of guilt, art and part in the murder, and on the ground that her statement to the police was inadmissible, having been unfairly obtained. This conviction related to her participation in an assault which resulted in the death of the victim. Earlier that evening she had participated in two other assaults where the men were robbed. Although each of these assaults had involved the use of weapons, neither involved murderous violence of the type used in the final assault.

The appellant had admitted kicking the deceased on the foot at the start of the attack. Evidence from blood stains on her clothing suggested she was near the deceased when he was punched while still standing. The court held that there was inadequate evidence to entitle the jury to convict the appellant of murder. Even if her statements were deemed admissible, the Court held that when the appellant had kicked the deceased at the start of the attack, there was no indication that she had reason to think that she was participating in a murderous attack. The Court also held that the appellant's statements that she kicked the deceased once on the feet at the start of the assault ought not to have been held to be admissible. The conviction was quashed.

The question of forseeability becomes more complex where, *e.g.* the carrying of some weapons forms part of the common plan but the fatal violence is done with a different weapon. In *O'Connell v. H.M. Advocate* (1987) four accused were convicted of murder. There was evidence that the common plan had involved the accused carrying sticks to use in their attack on the victim, however, a hammer belonging to the victim had been used to strike the fatal blow. The trial judge directed the jury that if the four accused formed a common plan to assault the victim with weapons that were capable of causing death or serious injury, or were aware that such weapons were likely to be used, then if in the course of that assault someone used another weapon which was of a similar type and capable of inflicting similar injury then all of the parties involved would be equally guilty as the man who inflicted the fatal blow. It was left to the jury to decide if a hammer was the same type of weapon as a stick. This direction was approved on appeal and the conviction confirmed. The liability of co-accused in such a scenario where a gun was used instead of sticks is less certain, however, this direction confirms that it would be for the jury to decide whether weapons are similar in respect of their capacity to inflict injury.

Where there are unintended consequences and the common purpose has arisen spontaneously, the test of forseeability is used. In these circumstances, however, where there is not a common plan, accused are more likely to be judged solely on their own actions.

Participation in an Ongoing Offence or after the Offence has been Committed.
If criminal activity is already under way when the accused participates, his criminal responsibility will only extend to the acts committed after his participation. He cannot be held responsible for any actions carried out before he participated. This situation is most likely to arise in respect of crimes of violence where, for example, the accused joins an individual or a group who are already assaulting the victim (see, *e.g. McLaughlan v. H.M. Advocate* (1991)).

Assistance or participation following the commission of a crime does not result in criminal responsibility for that crime. Assisting with the disposal of the stolen "getaway car" that has been used for a robbery will not, therefore, result in the helper being art and part guilty of robbery unless this was planned in advance of the robbery and was, therefore, part of the common plan. If no such plan existed and the hiding of car was only agreed after the robbery, the helper may be charged with reset (the retention of stolen goods), which is a separate offence.

Acquittal of Co-accused
A charge of art and part guilt can arise where all of the accused are principal offenders and also where only one or some of the accused are principal offenders and the others are accomplices. Where all of the accused are principal offenders it is possible for some to be convicted and others acquitted, *e.g. Capuano v. H.M. Advocate* (1984). Similarly, where there are principal and accomplice offenders it is possible for the principal to be convicted and the accomplice acquitted. Where, however, the crime is such that the participation of the principal offender is necessary for the commission of the offence and they have been acquitted, their accomplice will not be convicted. In *Young v. H.M. Advocate* (1932) Young and his co-accused, who were the directors and company secretary of a limited company, were charged with the fraudulent allotment of shares in that company. Young was convicted and his co-accused acquitted. On appeal his conviction was quashed because only people in the position of his co-accused could deal in the shares of the company. As they had been acquitted and he could not have acted on his own, his conviction was quashed.

Until recently it was assumed that the trial of one accused could not take place following the trial and acquittal of their co-accused, *e.g. McAuley v. H.M. Advocate* (1946), however, this has now been overruled by *Howitt v. H.M. Advocate*; *Duffy v. H.M. Advocate* (2000).

Omission and Art and Part Liability
Art and part liability can arise from a criminal omission, but only in those limited circumstances whereby a sole offender would be responsible for a criminal omission. The question of art and part responsibility for an omission tends to arise in circumstances where the co-accused is present during, but does not participate in, the commission of a crime. As there is no duty to prevent the commission of a crime in Scots law, this scenario does not generally lead to art and part guilt. However, in limited circumstances including where a co-accused is in a position of authority, criminal responsibility may arise from a failure to act. In *Bonar and Hogg v. MacLeod* (1983) the accused, a senior police officer, failed to intervene to prevent the assault of a prisoner in police custody, by an officer junior to himself. He was found to be art and part responsible for the assault. The common purpose presumably arose spontaneously here when the senior officer watched the junior officer assault the prisoner.

Outwith the special categories, where responsibility for criminal omissions arise, there will not be art and part guilt if an accused is merely present at the commission of a crime. In *H.M. Advocate v. Kerr*

(1871) three accused were charged with assault with intent to ravish. One of the accused, Donald, had not participated in the assault but had watched from the other side of a hedge in an adjoining field. Donald objected to the relevancy of the charge against him. Lord Ardmillan rejected the plea to the relevancy and ruled that the charge should go to the jury in order that all the circumstances be disclosed in evidence. He stated (at p. 337) that:

"It may be, that Donald actually encouraged the other prisoners by his language, or by his presence ... as to indicate readiness to give assistance, not to the girl but to her assailants, if necessary, and thus intimating the girl."

Lord Ardmillan directed the jury that as Donald was not in the field, but only looking through the hedge, it would not be safe to convict him.

Withdrawal from the Common Plan

The criminal responsibility of someone who withdraws from a common plan will depend on whether the accused withdraws at the preparation or perpetration stage. There are two conflicting public policy views on this. An individual should be able to change their mind once they have decided to embark on a criminal course but this must be balanced with the fact that a person cannot escape criminal liability when they have ensured that a crime took place by participating in its early stages, and have then left to avoid the consequences.

If there is withdrawal after the crime has started then the accused will not escape criminal liability. In *MacNeil v. H.M. Advocate* (1986) eight people were accused of drug smuggling by transporting drugs on board a ship from Nigeria to the U.K. The appellant and another accused left the ship when it arrived at a Spanish port. The appeal court differentiated between an accused who abandons a crime which is at the stage of preparation and one at the stage of perpetration. The Lord Justice-General (at p. 318) said:

"If a crime is merely in contemplation and preparations for it are being made, a participator who then quits the enterprise cannot be held to act in concert with those who may go on to commit the crime because there will be no evidence that he played any part in its commission. If, on the other hand, the perpetration of a planned crime or offence has begun, a participant cannot escape liability for the completed crime by withdrawing before it has been completed unless, perhaps, he also takes steps to prevent its completion."

The appeal was dismissed and the court emphasised that there was no defence of dissociation in Scots law. It is not clear from this judgment what lengths an accomplice would have to go to in order to prevent the completion of a crime, however, it should involve contacting the authorities.

INCHOATE CRIMES

Inchoate crimes are crimes where the *actus reus* has not been completed. Although criminal intention alone is never punished, it is not necessary that a crime be completed before the activity falls within prohibited behaviour. There are three specific crimes which deal with situations where the criminal activity falls short of a completed crime and these are known as inchoate crimes, they are: attempt, conspiracy and incitement.

ATTEMPT

All crimes may be attempted and any attempt to commit a crime is itself criminal (Criminal Procedure (Scotland) Act 1995, s.294). Why does the law penalise attempts? There are a number of possible reasons including; the criminal has clearly done her best to commit a crime but has been prevented from doing so by some external factor. This wickedness is viewed as being something that should be punished for both retributive and deterrence purposes.

An attempted crime comprises an *actus reus* and a *mens rea*. The *mens rea* will be identical to that of a completed crime. This is straightforward where the *mens rea* of the completed crime is intention, *e.g.* theft, however, problems arise when the *mens rea* of a crime is recklessness. Generally, Scots law does not recognise the possibility of a reckless attempt, as an essential part of the crime of attempt is that the accused intended to commit the crime which is libelled. The exception to this general rule is the law relating to attempted murder. In *McGregor v. H.M. Advocate* (1973) at p. 56 Lord Keith charged the jury as follows:

> "If you go out and recklessly fire off a firearm or wave a knife or dagger about and kill somebody, that may be murder. The test of attempted murder is whether, if the actions of the accused had resulted in the death of one of the [complainers] you would have said that was murder or not. If a man drives along with a policeman on his bonnet in such a way that the policeman falls off and is killed ... if you would have said that was murder, then you would be entitled to convict him [of attempted murder]".

Actus Reus

Whilst the *mens rea* of attempted crimes is relatively straightforward, a more difficult issue is the *actus reus*. Even if a crime is not completed, an accused can be said to have the requisite mental state for the *mens rea* of that crime. If the *actus reus* is not completed, however, it is necessary to determine the point at which the accused's activities become an attempt to commit a crime. When does a non-criminal preparation become an attempt at a crime? Intention alone is not enough, there must also be some conduct on the part of the accused which constitutes the crime and provides evidence of intention. No exact point in the perpetration of a crime has been identified in case law as amounting to the *actus reus* of an attempted crime. It is clear that merely forming the mental intention to commit a crime without further action is not enough (*H.M. Advocate v. MacKenzies* (1913)). Apart from this, however, case law is inconsistent and centres around three theories although it is not always clear which are being employed by the courts. There is evidence that the third of these theories has been preferred in more recent cases. The three theories are:

(1) irrevocability theory;
(2) last act theory; and
(3) perpetration theory.

(1) Irrevocability Theory

This theory suggests that a criminal attempt requires that the effect of the accused's actions must be irrevocable. In *H.M. Advocate v. Tannahill and Neilson* (1943) a partner in a firm of contractors was charged with attempting to induce sub-contractors, who had done work for him, to invoice a government department for this work, thereby attempting to defraud the government department. Lord Wark charged the jury (at p. 150) that: "As there was no evidence of any overt act on the part of the accused the consequences of which they could not recall, the jury were not entitled to convict of attempt to defraud." A verdict of not guilty was returned.

This approach results in criminal responsibility not arising until very late in the perpetration of a crime. It is obvious that if such an approach was universally adopted that this would produce difficulties for law enforcement and may also allow individuals to avoid criminal responsibility merely because of a chance intervention in their plans. More recent cases do not require that the situation has become irrevocable before criminal responsibility will arise.

(2) Last Act Theory

This theory is based on the idea that criminal liability for attempt will arise when the accused has done all that he believes is necessary to commit the proposed crime.

In the case of *Samuel Tumbelson* (1836) the accused was charged with attempting to poison his wife by giving a quantity of poisoned oatmeal to an innocent third party to give to his wife. An objection was taken to the relevancy of the indictment on the grounds that there was no averment that the poisoned oatmeal had reached or had been eaten by the woman or that the poisoned oatmeal had been placed beyond the control of the accused. Lord Neaves (at p. 430) said:

> "With regard to the second objection, it is true that the mere resolution to commit a crime is not indictable ... but when, as in the present case, machinery is put in motion, which, by its own nature is calculated to terminate in murder,– when this agency is let out of the party's hands to work its natural results,– that is a stage of the

operation by which he shows that he has completely developed in his own mind a murderous purpose, and has done all that in him lay to accomplish it."

The approach adopted in *Samuel Tumbelson* contradicts the first theory and, despite the early date of the case, adopts a stricter interpretation of the *actus reus* of attempt than is utilised in *H.M. Advocate v. Tannahill and Neilson (1943)*. If the last act theory is adopted it would result in criminal responsibility not arising until a fairly advanced stage of perpetration has been reached and this is no doubt why it is not the preferred approach in recent Scottish cases.

(3) Perpetration Theory
This third theory places a more onerous burden upon an accused, as it recognises a more flexible approach to the *actus reus* of attempt than the previous two theories. Perpetration theory is based on the premise that attempt involves any move, however slight, from preparation to perpetration. This appears to be the preferred approach in Scots law.

In *H.M. Advocate v. Camerons* (1911) a husband and wife were charged with the attempted fraud of an insurance company. They had insured a necklace as their own property although they only had temporary possession of it, staged a fake robbery and intimated this to their insurance broker. At their trial, the prosecution failed to prove that an insurance claim had been made although there was evidence of a letter by the accused to their insurance broker detailing the robbery. When directing the jury Lord Justice-General Dunedin (at p. 485) said that the essential question was where preparation ends and perpetration begins. He noted that this was a question of degree and it was a question that should be decided by the jury. He went on to say:

"The mere conceiving of the scheme—if you think a scheme was conceived—is not enough; but if that scheme is so carried out as that a false insurance is taken, and that a false robbery is gone through, very little more will do. At the same time you must remember that the actual claim has not been made."

The direction emphasised that the jury had to consider whether the actions of the accused had gone beyond the stage of preparation into the stage of perpetration. Both accused were found guilty.

This approach is clearly the most effective from a crime prevention and control perspective, however, it is not unproblematic. It is accepted that it is difficult for juries to determine when an accused has moved from mere preparation to the perpetration of a crime. This theory does provide a workable law of criminal attempts and perhaps a more precise definition of attempt is both impossible and impractical. This is illustrated by the fact that other jurisdictions apply an equally vague definition of attempt.

Attempting to do the Impossible
Attempting the impossible includes such scenarios as attempting to steal from a pocket that is empty. In this situation the accused intends to carry

out a particular crime and is prevented from doing so by some chance element. There was conflicting case law on this point until the decision in *Docherty v. Brown* (1996). Prior to *Docherty* an accused was convicted of attempted theft from an empty pocket in *Lamont v. Strathern* (1933). This decision conflicted with the approach by the courts in two cases, *H.M. Advocate v. Anderson* (1928) and *H.M. Advocate v. Semple* (1937), which each involved an accused charged with attempting to procure an abortion by supplying drugs to a woman that was believed to be pregnant. In each case the accused was acquitted as the recipient was not pregnant. Clearly the approach of the court in *Lamont* conflicted with that in *Anderson* and *Semple*. The five bench decision in *Docherty v. Brown (1996)* has clarified that, in Scots law, impossibility does not act as a defence to a charge of attempt.

In *Docherty*, the appellant had been convicted of possession of drugs with intent to supply, contrary to the Misuse of Drugs Act 1971. The appellant had mistakenly believed that the tablets in his possession contained a controlled drug. This was incorrect and the tablets were in fact harmless. The appeal was refused. The account of the law by Lord Justice-Clerk Ross received the support of three of the other judges. He noted (at p. 60) that:

"For a relevant charge of an attempt to commit a crime, it must be averred that the accused had the necessary *mens rea*, and that he has done some positive act towards executing his purpose, that is to say that he has done something which amounts to perpetration rather than mere preparation. If what is libelled is an attempt to commit a crime which is impossible of achievement, impossibility is irrelevant except that there can be no attempt to commit the crime if the accused is aware that what he is trying to do is impossible."

This decision clarified that the previous distinction between legal and factual impossibility is no longer an issue in impossible attempts, however, where an accused mistakenly attempts an action which they believe to be criminal but it is in fact legal, no criminal responsibility will arise.

CONSPIRACY

A conspiracy requires the intentional agreement of two or more people to commit a crime (*Maxwell v. H.M. Advocate* (1980)). The *mens rea* of this offence is intention and the *actus reus* is agreement to commit a crime. Nothing else needs to be done in pursuance of that agreement for a crime to have been committed, however, it will be difficult to prove a conspiracy unless there is evidence indicating that such an agreement was reached (*Sayers v. H.M. Advocate* (1981)). A conspiracy charge may libel that specific crimes were carried out in pursuance of the conspiracy, but where the indictment is more vague and merely refers to a conspiracy to achieve a purpose by criminal means it is necessary that the criminal means be specified or the charge will be held to be irrelevant (*Sayers v. H.M. Advocate* (1981)).

While individuals are often charged, both with conspiring to commit a crime and the completed crime, it is not competent to convict an accused of both. The reasons for charging both include that it allows evidence relating to events leading up to the commission of the crime to be considered by the court and also, that it increases the chances of conviction as it may be easier to prove a conspiracy to commit a crime rather than the completed crime. An objection to the competency of charging both conspiracy to murder and murder was argued in a preliminary diet of "the Lockerbie trial" (*H.M. Advocate v. Al Megrahi* (2000)). This preliminary plea was refused by Lord Sutherland (at p. 189D–F).

Proving Conspiracy
In conspiracy cases it is unlikely that a witness will be available who can speak to agreement being reached between the accused. As a consequence, evidence of a conspiracy will be inferred from the actions of the accused. In *West v. H.M. Advocate* (1985) the accused were charged with conspiring to assault and rob employees who worked in a particular building. The charge narrated that, in furtherance of the conspiracy, the accused

"did loiter in the vicinity of said premises ... and thereafter enter the said premises while ... in possession of a blade from a pair of scissors, and ... in possession of an open razor, all with intent to assault said employees with said weapons and rob them of money."

On appeal it was held that there was sufficient evidence from which to infer a conspiracy.

Conspiring to do the Impossible
The approach adopted by the courts to conspiring to do the impossible, mirrors that adopted in relation to impossible attempts. As noted above, the crime of conspiracy is committed when two individuals agree to commit a crime and, therefore, the fact that some intervening event would make the completion of the crime impossible is irrelevant. In *Maxwell v. H.M. Advocate* (1980) Lord Cameron directed that, since conspiracy involved the agreement to achieve a criminal purpose, it was the criminality of that agreement and not the result which makes the activity criminal. Impossibility is, therefore, irrelevant.

Withdrawal as a Defence?
Where two individuals have agreed to a criminal purpose, they have committed the crime of conspiracy. As a result, at the point of agreement the crime of conspiracy is complete and there is no opportunity to withdraw. It would be possible for an accused to have abandoned the criminal purpose at a later point, however, this may affect

her responsibility for either the attempted crime or the completed crime but she would still have conspired to commit the crime.

INCITEMENT

A person who invites another to participate in the commission of a crime is guilty of incitement. The crime is committed as soon as the invitation is made and is not dependent on the invitation being accepted. Indeed if the invitation is accepted, the crime would then be one of conspiracy rather than incitement. The *mens rea* of incitement is the intention that the incited party commit the relevant crime and the *actus reus* is the invitation.

INCITEMENT, CONSPIRACY AND ART AND PART GUILT

Each of the above are potentially stages in the commission of a crime where more than one person is involved. Incitement involves one person inviting another to participate in a criminal purpose. If this invitation is accepted, then at that point, the two (or more) parties are described as conspiring to commit the crime. If either or both go on to commit the crime then they will be regarded as art and part liable in the commission of the crime, due to their common plan.

READING

P. W. Ferguson, *Crimes Against the Person* (2nd ed., Butterworths, Edinburgh, 1998), Chap. 12.

C. Gane, C. Stoddart and J. Chalmers, *A Casebook on Scottish Criminal Law* (3rd ed., W. Green & Son, Edinburgh, 2001), Chaps 2–6.

G. H. Gordon, *Criminal Law* (3rd ed., M. Christie (ed.), W. Green & Son, Edinburgh, 2000), Vol. I, Chaps 3–9.

T. Jones and M. Christie, *Criminal Law* (2nd ed., W. Green & Son, Edinburgh, 1996), Vol. I, Chaps 3–7.

R. McCall Smith and D. Sheldon, *Scots Criminal Law* (Butterworths, Edinburgh, 1997), Chaps 2–7.

3. CRIMES AGAINST THE PERSON

NON SEXUAL OFFENCES AGAINST THE PERSON

ASSAULT

The crime of assault can be described as an intentional attack upon the person of another. The *actus reus* of assault is an attack upon the person and the *mens rea* is intention.

Actus Reus of Assault

The *actus reus* of assault has been interpreted widely by the courts and has been held to include attacks which do not result in injury, indirect attacks and even words where no violence is used. The use of physical violence in the course of a "fight" is probably closest to the popular understanding of assault. While this would amount to an assault, other types of behaviour are also included in the definition. Case law indicates that any degree of violence that is deliberate fulfils the legal definition of assault, *e.g.* putting paper in someone's hand and setting fire to it (*Lachlan Brown* (1842)) and twisting someone's hand behind their back (*Codona v. Cardle* (1989)). Harm does not require to be caused to the victim and, therefore, aimed blows or missiles which miss the intended victim may still be held to constitute an assault (*Stewart v. Procurator Fiscal of Forfarshire* (1829)).

The assault may not even involve direct contact between the accused and the victim. In *Quinn v. Lees* (1994) the accused was charged with setting his dog on three boys by giving the dog the command "fetch". The accused claimed that this was done as a joke. As the dog was held to be unable to distinguish between a command and a joke, the accused was held to have carried out a deliberate act with predictable consequences. An assault can also be committed by making threatening gestures that place the victim in a state of fear and alarm. In *Atkinson v. H.M. Advocate* (1987) the Appeal Court confirmed an assault conviction of a man who entered a shop with his face masked and jumped over the counter to where the cashier was standing. The Appeal Court held that an assault may be constituted by threatening gestures that are sufficient to produce alarm.

The *Mens Rea* of Assault

Assault is a crime of intent in Scots law and, therefore, cannot be committed recklessly or negligently. The *mens rea* of assault was described by MacDonald as "evil intent". The definition of "evil intent" was, until recently, expressed as "intent to injure and do bodily harm" (see Lord Justice-General Wheatley in *Smart v. H.M. Advocate* (1975), p. 33).

The definition of "evil intent" has been clarified in the leading modern authority on the question, *Lord Advocate's Reference (No. 2 of 1992)* (1992). In this case the accused was charged with assault with attempt to rob and attempted robbery. He had entered a shop, pointed an imitation gun towards the owner and asked for the contents of the till. When he realised that there were other people in the shop, the accused ran out. In his evidence the accused said that his actions were a joke. The jury were directed that if they believed the accused had no evil intent, they should acquit him. The jury acquitted the accused and the Lord Advocate referred the case to the High Court to determine whether the accused's evidence did amount to a defence to a charge of assault. In his opinion Lord Justice-Clerk Ross stated (at p. 965):

"It has often been said that evil intention is of the essence of assault ... But what that means is that assault cannot be committed accidentally or recklessly or negligently ... In the present case, it is plain that when the accused entered the shop, presented the handgun at Mrs Daly and uttered the words which he did, he was acting deliberately. That being so, in my opinion he had the necessary intent for his actions to amount to assault, and his motive for acting as he did was irrelevant. I agree with the advocate-depute that the principle laid down by the Lord Justice-Clerk in *H.M. Advocate v. Edmiston* would apply to the present case and that, even if the accused was believed when he stated it was a joke, his acting as he did would still constitute the crime of assault."

Lord Cowie emphasises the importance of the term evil in "evil intention". At p. 968 he states in relation to the requirements for the crime of assault that "having established that the act is an evil one, all that is then required to constitute the crime of assault is that that act was done deliberately and not carelessly, recklessly or negligently". Similarly Lord Sutherland makes particular reference to both "evil" and "intention" in his opinion. At pp. 969–970 he states:

"The words 'evil intent' have an eminently respectable pedigree ... It is, however, perfectly possible to have an intention to perform particular acts without necessarily intending evil consequences from those acts. If intention means motive then plainly it is irrelevant. If, on the other hand, intention means nothing more than wilful, intentional or deliberate as opposed to accidental, careless or even reckless, then plainly it is relevant in that a criminal act cannot be performed other than deliberately ... If, therefore, a person deliberately performs an act which would in itself be criminal then both the *actus reus* and the *mens rea* coexist and a crime has been committed."

Evil intent is clearly still regarded as being the *mens rea* of assault and there is consensus that the intention represents a deliberate action.

There is not a concise and agreed definition of evil, however, it does still play a role in distinguishing situations where there is clearly intentional bodily harm inflicted in the context of, *e.g.* sport compared with that inflicted in a physical fight. Both cases involve intention, however, violence done during sport will not be regarded as criminal as it remains within the rules of the game, whereas the violence in a physical fight is capable of being "evilly intended" and, therefore, an assault.

Where the requisite intention for assault is absent, it is open to the prosecutor to charge, *e.g.* causing reckless injury or causing real injury as in the case of *Khaliq v. H.M. Advocate* (1984). This must, however, be libelled and will not be available as an alternative verdict to a charge of assault (see *H.M. Advocate v. Harris* (1993) and the earlier section on "transferred intent" in Chapter 2).

Reflex Actions
As the crime of assault requires that the accused's actions are both voluntary and deliberate it has been assumed that actions that are neither of these, *e.g.* reflex actions, fall outwith the scope of the crime. The classification of actions as "reflex" has received little attention in reported cases with the exception of *Jessop v. Johnstone* (1991). The accused, a school gym teacher, was hit on the nose with a rolled up school jotter by a 14-year-old male pupil. He responded instantly with blows to the pupil's stomach and back. The teacher was charged with assault and at his trial the sheriff acquitted him. The prosecution appealed against this acquittal. The sheriff was of the view that the teacher had acted immediately and spontaneously and did not have the requisite *mens rea* of evil intent required to be convicted of assault. The prosecution appealed successfully and the High Court directed that a conviction be returned, saying *inter alia*, that the sheriff had confused provocation with absence of intent. Lord Justice-Clerk Ross stated (at p. 240):
> "We appreciate that there may be cases where a person instinctively reacts to violence in a reflex way, such as if a person is suddenly and without warning struck and turns round sharply so that he comes into contact with his assailant. The present case, however, clearly did not fall within that category at all because it is plain ... that the (teacher) jumped up and struck the complainer more than once ... on both the stomach and back."

The court indicated that the sheriff might find that the teacher had been provoked if the evidence supported the requirements of that defence.

Attempted Assault
As the *actus reus* of the crime of assault has been interpreted very widely, the question of an attempted assault does not arise. Remember that no harm need be inflicted for the requirement of an "attack upon the person of another" to be fulfilled. Therefore, attempts at physically

hitting or alarming a person will fulfil the *actus reus* of assault even if
the perpetrator does not carry out every aspect of the attack as intended.

Serious Assault

Serious assaults are generally referred to as aggravated assaults. A
number of different factors can result in an assault being aggravated.
The *mens rea* of an aggravated assault is in many cases identical to an
assault, namely, evil intention. This varies, however, in some cases, for
example, where knowledge that the person assaulted is a police officer,
is necessary for the aggravated assault of "assault of a police officer"
(see *Annan v. Tait* (1982)). The *actus reus* is "an attack upon the person
of another", however, characteristics of the victim or how the attack is
delivered may serve to aggravate an assault.

Any feature of an assault may serve to aggravate the offence and the
following are merely examples. Some of these are described as statutory
aggravations, *i.e.* it is the provisions of a statute which dictate that the
assault is aggravated in the circumstances and others are common law
aggravations.

Statutory aggravations include assault of a police officer (s.41,
Police (Scotland) Act 1967) where the accused must know or reasonably
believe that the person is a police officer and racial aggravations (s.96,
Crime and Disorder Act 1998) which makes it an offence either at the
time of commission, or immediately before, to evince malice or ill-will
towards the victim on the basis of their membership, or presumed
membership, of a racial group. There are also statutory aggravations
relating to lewdness and indecency contained within the Sexual
Offences (Scotland) Act 1976.

Common law aggravations include the method of perpetration, *e.g.*
where a weapon is used, "assault with a weapon"; where serious injury
is caused, *e.g.* "assault to severe injury" or "assault to the danger of
life", or where there are circumstances of lewdness or indecency, *e.g.*
"indecent assault".

Justified Assault

If an assault is justified it will no longer be regarded as criminal
behaviour. Some forms of violence are justified if they occur, *e.g.* as
part of a war, and the foundation of that justification is public policy.
Three types of justification are recognised by the criminal law, namely:

(1) justification by public policy;
(2) justification by the victim's conduct; and
(3) justification by the victim's consent.

(1) Justification by Public Policy

Certain types of violence are authorised by the state in particular
contexts. So we can see that the force or violence used by a police

officer in securing an arrest is justified so long as it is not excessive. If it is excessive it becomes an assault. A private citizen may use reasonable force to secure a citizen's arrest where a serious crime has been committed, however, they must have witnessed the crime being committed or have equivalent information as to the identity of the perpetrator. Where excessive force is used in securing such an arrest this will be treated as an assault (*Codona v. Cardle* (1989)). The public policy reasons for restricting a citizen's right to take on the role of the police in crime detection is obvious.

It remains the law in Scotland that parents can physically chastise their children so long as they use moderate and reasonable force. At the time of writing, the Scottish Executive were considering making the physical chastisement of children under three years of age a crime. There are cases where parents have been convicted of assault of their child because the necessary *mens rea* as evidenced by excessive force was used (*Pebbles v. McPhail* (1990)) In other cases the court has held that the loss of temper by a parent does not necessarily allow the *mens rea* of "evil intent" to be inferred. In *Guest v. Annan* (1988) the appellant was charged with assaulting his eight-year-old daughter by repeatedly striking her on the buttocks, to her injury. The father had lost his temper after his daughter lied to him about where she had been and the repeated smacking resulted in the girl bruising. He was convicted, but on appeal the High Court quashed the conviction saying that the loss of temper and displeasure with his daughter did not automatically mean that the father had the necessary *mens rea* of "evil intent" for the crime of assault. The use of excessive force by a parent may also contravene section 12(1) of the Children and Young Persons (Scotland) Act 1937 which prohibits a parent "causing or procuring the assault of their child" and Article 3 of the Convention which provides that noone shall be subjected to torture or inhuman or degrading treatment or punishment.

In each of the above cases it is clear that the courts do not only look at whether the necessary *mens rea* and *actus reus* are present but also whether the force used is reasonable. This will be decided on the circumstances of the case and in all scenarios if excessive force is used it is no longer justified, but will be treated as an assault in its own right. For example, in *Bonar and Hogg v. Macleod* (1983) the High Court held that a police officer who grasped an arrested person by the throat, twisted his arm up his back and "quick marched" him down a corridor had used excessive force in view of the fact that the prisoner was neither resisting arrest nor struggling with the officer at the time. Both the police officer and his supervising officer who witnessed this were convicted art and part of assault.

(2) Justification by the Victim's Conduct
If, while acting in their own or a third party's defence, an individual behaves in a way that would otherwise constitute an assault, so long as the rules of self-defence are complied with, these actions will not be regarded as an assault (*H.M. Advocate v. Carson* (1964)). This is

because the person is acting to protect themselves or a third party and does not have the requisite *mens rea* of evil intention that is required for the crime of assault. The rules of self-defence are outlined in Chapter 6. It should be noted that where the rules are not met and, in particular, where any retaliation is excessive the defending actions will be regarded as an assault (*Moore v. MacDougall* (1989)).

The limited Scottish authority on the question of using force in defence of property suggests that self-defence is not available as a defence where there is savage excess and the degree of violence is disproportionate to need (*H.M. Advocate v. Robertson and Donoghue* (1945)). Self-defence in respect of property was unsuccessfully pled in the English case *Martin v. R.* (2001) where the accused was convicted of murder and grievous bodily harm when he shot at two retreating intruders, killing one and seriously injuring the other. At appeal this conviction was reduced to manslaughter on the grounds that he was suffering from diminished responsibility. The three Appeal Court judges sentenced him to five years' imprisonment.

(3) Justification by the Victim's Consent
The question of whether a victim's consent to an assault would serve to elide criminal responsibility was considered in the case *Smart v. H.M. Advocate* (1975). In *Smart* the accused was convicted of assaulting a person by kicking, punching and biting. His defence at trial was essentially that his actions could not amount to assault as the victim had accepted his invitation to a "square go", *i.e.* a physical fight. He also claimed that his actions were in self-defence. The sheriff had directed the jury that consent was not a defence to assault and that there was no evidence to support a plea of self-defence. The jury convicted Smart and he appealed on the grounds that consent was a defence to assault, and so the sheriff had misdirected the jury.

The Appeal Court refused the appeal and in their judgment clarified the following:

(a)   Consent is not a defence to a charge of assault even where the two parties have agreed to fight. Similarly consent is not recognised as a defence to a charge of murder (*H.M. Advocate v. Rutherford* (1947)).

(b)   Consent is available as a defence to a charge of indecent assault because in those circumstances where consent is present and there is no other criminal activity the perpetrator lacks the necessary *mens rea* of evil intent. This can be distinguished from a physical fight where, even if there is consent to fight, the perpetrator still has the necessary evil intent when inflicting injury on their opponent.

(c)   Sporting activities which involve a degree of violence, *e.g.* rugby or boxing, will not be regarded as amounting to an assault where any physical injury is within the rules of the game. This is justified on the basis that the sporting competitor lacks the necessary *mens rea* of evil intent when acting within the rules of the game. The intention is to compete in the game rather than to inflict injury on the opponent and, therefore, the necessary *mens rea* for the crime of assault is missing. In distinguishing sporting activities from a "square go" the court noted (at p. 66) that "where the whole purpose of the exercise is to inflict physical damage on the opponent in pursuance of a quarrel then the evil intent is present and consent is elided."

The distinction between sporting activities, *e.g.* boxing, and a "square go" may be difficult to sustain unless one accepts that public policy considerations may have some bearing on the distinctions drawn by the Court in their judgment.

Provocation and Assault
Provocation may serve to mitigate the punishment of an accused convicted of assault. While the rules of provocation are fully explored in Chapter 6, an exception to the rules will be considered here. In respect of homicide only physical provocation is recognised, however, in respect of the crime of assault both verbal and physical provocation is recognised. Any verbal provocation requires to be inflammatory abuse which leads to an immediate loss of self-control (*Thomson v. H.M. Advocate* (1985)). A successful plea of provocation to a charge of assault does not result in the acquittal of the accused but instead serves to mitigate the punishment given.

RECKLESS CONDUCT

Reckless conduct crimes occur where harm or injury is inflicted on the victim, or a dangerous situation is created, and the accused lacks the *mens rea* of intention. Where the perpetrator has acted negligently or accidentally there will be no criminal responsibility. It is only where the actions involve a *mens rea* of recklessness that they will be categorised as a reckless conduct crime. Examples of these offences are considered below.

CRUEL AND BARBAROUS TREATMENT AND CRUEL AND UNNATURAL TREATMENT

Both of these offences involve neglect or cruel treatment of a person for whom the perpetrator is responsible. This charge was more commonly found in nineteenth-century indictments prior to, *e.g.* children being protected by statute including the Children and Young Persons (Scotland) Act 1937. The charge has arisen more recently, however, in respect of a nun who was charged with the cruel and unnatural treatment of people who had been in her care in two orphanages when they were children (*Higson (Procurator Fiscal of Aberdeen) v. Docherty*, September 2000, Aberdeen Sheriff Court, unreported).

CAUSING REAL INJURY

Hume (i, 327) noted that, where in an indictment, terms such as assault or stabbing are not used but the conduct described nevertheless amounts to conduct which would cause real injury to a person, then that shall be treated as a criminal act no matter how new or strange the wrong. This passage from Hume could clearly apply to a wide variety of circumstances. It was relied upon in the case *Khaliq v. H.M. Advocate* (1984) which involved the supply of noxious substances by the accused, in the knowledge that they would be used in a way that was injurious to the recipients health.

In *Khaliq*, the two accused were charged on indictment that they had culpably, wilfully and recklessly supplied to a number of children "glue-sniffing kits" in the knowledge of how they would be used, the dangers associated with this and that they did cause or procure the children to inhale the vapours from the solvents to the danger of their health and lives. The second charge was one of reset and related to stolen goods that had been exchanged for the "glue-sniffing kits". A preliminary plea to the relevancy of both charges was refused and leave was given to appeal. At both the initial hearing and the appeal of the preliminary plea the Court confirmed that the first charge was a crime known to the law of Scotland and referred to the above passage from Hume. The Lord Justice-General (Lord Emslie) said (at p. 143) referring to Hume (i, 327):
    "The general principle to be discovered from this passage is that within the category of conduct identified as criminal are acts, whatever their nature may be, which cause real injury to the person. Does this case, though never before occurring on its facts, fall within that general principle ... ? In my opinion it does".
The opinion of the Court also states that the consent of the victim, in their action of inhaling the substance, does not elide the criminal responsibility of the accused. The age of the children was not held to be essential to the relevancy of the charge, but would be relevant in determining whether the supply complained of ought to be held to have been a cause of the injury suffered. The Court also considered whether there was a causal link between the actions of the accused and the harm suffered. This is discussed in more detail in Chapter 2.

The requisite *actus reus* and *mens rea* of this crime is not clear in *Khaliq*, however, the direction to the jury in *Ulhaq v. H.M. Advocate* (1990) defines what is required in the context of supply of noxious substances. The accused in *Ulhaq* was charged with essentially the same crime as had arisen in *Khaliq*. The charge was one of
    "culpably and recklessly endangering the lives and health of a number of people in their twenties by selling them a substantial quantity of various solvents, knowing that the recipients intended to use them for inhaling their vapours and that such inhalation would be injurious to their health, and to the danger of their lives, and

with causing or procuring said inhalation to the danger of the recipients' health and lives." (p. 593)

The jury were directed that the crime charged required proof that there was the culpable, wilful and reckless supply of certain items for the purpose of abuse, and that these were supplied in the knowledge of how they were to be used and that this would be injurious to health and to the danger of their lives.

Presumably, the *actus reus* of this crime could be fulfilled by a variety of means including supply and administration. There is no requirement for "an attack" which is necessary for the crime of assault. While this is a crime of recklessness the direction to the jury in *Ulhaq* focuses on the knowledge of the accused both of the purpose for which the substances are to be used and the effect of their use.

RECKLESS INJURY

This crime involves unintentionally but recklessly causing injury to another. In *H.M. Advocate v. Harris* (1993) the accused, a night-club bouncer, was charged with assaulting a woman to her severe injury and permanent disfigurement by seizing hold of her, pushing her on the body and causing her to fall down a flight of stairs and onto a roadway as a result of which she was struck by a passing motorvehicle. There was an alternative charge of culpably, wilfully and recklessly seizing hold of the woman, pushing her on the body and causing her to fall down a flight of stairs and onto the roadway as a result of which she was struck by a motorvehicle to her severe injury and permanent disfigurement. An objection to the relevancy of the alternative charge was sustained by the sheriff and thereafter successfully appealed by the Crown to the High Court. A bench of five judges held that a charge of reckless conduct did not require to be libelled as being "to the danger of the lieges" before it was relevant and thereby overruled the decision in *Quinn v. Cunningham* (1956). The Court also rejected the submission that both charges libelled the same crime and were therefore not truly alternatives. The Court held, by majority, with Lord McCluskey dissenting, that, although the same conduct was libelled in both charges, they were distinguished by the *mens rea* required for each crime, *i.e.* assault requires intent whereas reckless conduct/injury requires a *mens rea* of recklessness. Lord McCluskey dissenting said (at p. 969K–L):

"[W]here one has got an averment of wilful seizing of a person and pushing her on the body thereby causing her to fall down a flight of stairs there is absolutely no need to invent and innominate crime. The familiar crime of assault fits the bill perfectly … In my opinion, the alternative charge in the indictment is irrelevant on the ground that it does not disclose a crime known to the law of Scotland. In my opinion, there is no crime known to the law of Scotland consisting of wilfully seizing another human being, pushing her on the body and causing her to fall down a flight of stairs, except the crime of assault. As *ex hypothesi* the alternative charge does not contain a charge of assault it cannot be relevant."

RECKLESSLY ENDANGERING THE LIEGES

This crime is distinguishable from reckless injury in that it will be charged where an accused has created a dangerous situation that may have placed the public in danger, even although no actual injury has been caused. The dangerous situation can be the result of the reckless performing of either a lawful or an unlawful act. Many cases in this category involve the reckless discharge of firearms, *e.g.* in *Cameron v. Maguire* (1999) the offence is libelled as "you did recklessly discharge a loaded rifle in the direction of open woodland to the danger of the lieges who might reasonably be expected to be walking there." However, other types of behaviour have been libelled as recklessly endangering the lieges, *e.g.* "culpably and recklessly promoting and organising a rave in a derelict warehouse to the danger of the lieges" in *Normand v. Robinson* (1994).

HOMICIDE

Actus Reus
Two types of homicide are recognised in Scots law; murder and culpable homicide. The *actus reus* of both murder and culpable homicide is the destruction of human life other than one's own. There is no time-limit within which death must result, however, there must be a causal connection between the actions of the accused and the harm suffered. As there is no time-limit, an accused who has been convicted of assaulting his victim may also be prosecuted at a later date for murder or culpable homicide should the victim subsequently die from the injuries inflicted. The principle of *res judicata* will not apply to such a scenario and prevent the additional prosecution for the new crime.

It is necessary for a charge of homicide that life is actually destroyed. Although there is not a legal definition of death, it is assumed to involve the permanent cessation of all brain activity. For life to have been destroyed it is necessary that the victim of homicide had been alive. This means that a child must be born and have a separate existence of it's own before it is regarded as a living human being. Where death is caused by injures received in the womb, so long as the child has lived for a short time outside the womb, it will be relevant to charge murder or culpable homicide in respect of the injuries. If the child does not survive outside the womb, then the perpetrator could only be charged with a crime related to injuring the pregnant woman.

A further requirement is that the life taken must be other than one's own. Although suicide and attempted suicide are not crimes in Scotland, where one person kills another as part of a "suicide pact" and then survives, they have fulfilled the legal requirements for the crime of murder, but in practice will be charged with culpable homicide.

Differences Between Murder and Culpable Homicide

As noted above, the *actus reus* of murder and culpable homicide is identical. The crimes are distinguished by the punishment and the *mens rea*. In all common law crimes, except murder, the punishment is at the discretion of the sentencer within the statutory limits that are laid down. In the case of murder, the punishment is a mandatory life sentence, whereas for culpable homicide, the sentence is at the discretion of the judge. The *mens rea* of each crime differ and are explored below.

Prior to exploring the *mens rea* of each crime, it should be noted that not all deaths result in a charge of murder or culpable homicide. Where the actions of the accused are negligent or accidental this will not result in a charge of murder nor culpable homicide as the accused lacks the necessary *mens rea*. As noted in Chapter 2, negligence is not a recognised form of *mens rea*. Accidental or negligent homicide is often referred to as casual homicide. Alison defined casual homicide as:

"[W]here a person kills unintentionally, when lawfully employed, and neither meaning harm to anyone, nor having failed in the due degree of care and circumspection for preventing mischief to his neighbour." (*Criminal Law*, Vol. I, pp. 139–140)

An example is given of where a person's gun burst in his hand and kills his neighbour.

Where the killing of another person is deemed to be justified, the law will treat such actions as non-criminal homicides. Homicide can be justified by a number of factors including, death caused by the armed forces which occur in the context of war, or where a person acting in self-defence kills an attacker. The requirements of self-defence are examined in Chapter 6.

Mens Rea of Murder

The classic definition of the crime of murder is given by MacDonald as:

"[M]urder is constituted by a wilful act causing the destruction of life, whether intended to kill, or displaying such wicked recklessness as to imply a disposition depraved enough to be regardless of the consequences." (*A Practical Treatise on the Criminal Law of Scotland* (5th ed., 1948), p. 89)

It is generally accepted that there are two forms of *mens rea* for the crime of murder. These are intention and wicked recklessness. As in all other crimes, the *mens rea* of the accused will be inferred from the circumstances. Therefore, although murder is a result crime, *i.e.* we are interested in the result of the actions of the accused and not the conduct, the conduct will give us an insight into the *mens rea* of the accused.

Wicked Intention

The *mens rea* of any crime is the mental state of the accused at the time the crime was committed. As a consequence, motive and premeditation are not relevant. Intention is, therefore, judged at the time the act was committed. MacDonald and the majority of case law refer to the *mens rea* of murder as "intention". While this continued to be viewed as a correct statement of the law, two recent cases have suggested a variation. In the case *Fenning v. H.M. Advocate* (1985) Lord Mayfield directed the jury that they could not convict of murder if there was an absence of "wicked intent or recklessness" (at p. 220). In a more recent case, *Drury v. H.M. Advocate* (2001), a bench of five judges held that the *mens rea* of murder was "wicked intention" which departs from both MacDonald's definition and the mere "intention" which has been referred to in other cases. The adoption of "wicked intention" as the *mens rea* of murder will have wider implications than merely challenging prior understandings. Christie (2001) suggests that the opinions in Drury may be read to suggest that wickedness requires to be proven or admitted intention to kill. The onus for proving wickedness will rest upon the prosecutor and failure to do so or indeed the accused convincing a jury that her intention was not wicked should lead to acquittal. Christie submits that a jury should be advised that the *mens rea* of murder is a wicked intent to kill but that if they are satisfied that the accused intended to kill, they may infer that the accused had a wicked intention in the absence of any legally relevant factor, *e.g.* provocation.

Christie's submission in respect of jury direction would prevent a possible and surely unintended consequence of the decision in *Drury*, namely that it would serve to distinguish so called "mercy killings", *i.e.* where the victim wishes to be killed to be relieved from suffering, from acts of violence that are neither invited nor consensual. The absence of "wicked intent" in the former scenario would prohibit "mercy killings" from being classified as murder. Other commentators have also suggested that the effect of *Drury* is limited. Gane and Stoddart (2001) suggest that it may be limited to those cases where the accused presents excusing or justifying factors (in the form of criminal defences, *e.g.* provocation) to the court and argues that these serve to negate the "wickedness" required for murder.

Consent, Intention and Murder
The general rule in criminal law that a person cannot consent to harm being done to them, is followed in respect of both murder and culpable homicide. In *H.M. Advocate v. Rutherford* (1947) the accused was charged with murder of a woman. He gave evidence that the woman had requested that he strangle her with his tie and that she had put the tie around her neck. He told the Court that he had pulled the tie and, on the woman telling him to get on with it, he had pulled it again. He said that he had not intended to harm the woman but only to frighten or humour her. When he discovered she was dead he had reported the matter to the police. Under cross-examination he admitted that he must have used a strong pull of the neck-tie and that he was aware that such actions involved a good chance of choking the victim to death. Medical evidence referred to the presence of both tie marks and hand marks on the woman's neck with the latter being consistent with manual

strangling. Lord Justice-Clerk Cooper directed the jury to reject the defence submission that the actions of the accused amounted to casual homicide. On the question of the consent of the victim he said (at pp. 5–6):

"[I]f life is taken under circumstances which would otherwise infer guilt of murder, the crime does not cease to be murder merely because the victim consented to be murdered, or even urged the assailant to strike the fatal blow ... The attitude of the victim is irrelevant. What matters is the intent of the assailant."

Despite this the jury returned a unanimous verdict of culpable homicide.

The consent of the victim has not reduced the responsibility of a person who kills to relieve the victim from suffering or who survives a suicide pact having killed the other party. In both instances the perpetrator has demonstrated the necessary intention required for the crime of murder although in practice this is prosecuted as culpable homicide. As noted above, it is presumed that this has not been altered by the decision in *Drury*.

Intention to do Serious Bodily Harm

Reference to the existence of a second form of intentional *mens rea* for the crime of murder, namely, "intention to do serious bodily harm", has been referred to in some cases including *H.M. Advocate v. Hartley* (1989) and *H.M. Advocate v. Cawthorne* (1968). This is now largely accepted as being an error. Note, however, that the seriousness of injuries inflicted may assist in drawing an inference of the intention to kill.

Wicked Recklessness

As noted above, there are only two *mens rea* of murder, namely, wicked intention and wicked recklessness. The case of *H.M. Advocate v. Cawthorne* (1968) confirmed wicked recklessness as a separate *mens rea* for the crime of murder. Wicked recklessness can be inferred in cases where the accused does not have a deliberate intention to kill but acts with such wicked recklessness as to show that they are indifferent as to whether or not death results. Thus, wicked recklessness requires something more than mere recklessness which has been defined as "a total indifference to and disregard for the safety of the public." *(RHW v. H.M. Advocate* (1982), p. 420). Hume suggests that there are three requirements for this form of *mens rea*:

(1) the accused should have meant to perpetrate some great and outrageous bodily harm;

(2) the harm was such as might well have resulted in death; and

(3) the harm showed an absolute or utter indifference as to whether the victim lived or died. (*Commentaries on the Law of Scotland Respecting Crimes* (4th ed., by B.R. Bell, reprinted 1986), Vol. I, pp. 191, 238 and 256)

The *mens rea* of wicked recklessness usually arises when death occurs in the course of another serious crime. In these cases an element of violence will be involved. It is sometimes, incorrectly, assumed that the use of weapons in the perpetration of any crime where death occurs will result in a charge of murder. This assumption may be partly attributable to the direction to the jury by Lord Justice-Clerk Aitchison in *H.M. Advocate v. McGuinness* ((1937), p. 40) that:

"people who use knives and pokers and hatchets against a fellow citizen are not entitled to say 'we did not mean to kill', if death results. If people resort to the use of deadly weapons of this kind, they are guilty of murder, whether or not they intended to kill."

This is not wholly accurate as the use of these weapons allow an inference to be drawn that the accused meant to perpetrate some great and outrageous bodily harm, that the harm was such as might well have resulted in death and that the harm showed an absolute or utter indifference as to whether the victim lived or died. The question in these circumstances is whether the *mens rea* for murder can be inferred from all of the circumstances, including the use of weapons.

Traditionally in Scots law, where death occurred during the perpetration of other serious crimes, *e.g.* rape, abortion and robbery, this was deemed to be the crime of murder regardless of the *mens rea* of the accused or the level of violence involved. Modern case law has departed from this assumption and now requires evidence of *mens rea*. In some relatively recent cases (*H.M. Advocate v. Fraser and Rollins* (1920) and *H.M. Advocate v. Miller and Denovan* (unreported, see Gane and Stoddart, p. 404), there has been reference to the so-called "constructive murder rule" applying to the crime of robbery. In these cases, however, there is adequate evidence from which the *mens rea* of wicked recklessness can be inferred.

Mens Rea of Culpable Homicide

The *mens rea* of culpable homicide is recklessness. The crime of culpable homicide has been described by MacDonald as a crime where death is caused by improper conduct but the guilt is less than murder. Where an accused is charged with murder and successfully pleads a mitigating defence, *e.g.* provocation, they will be convicted of culpable homicide. The crime of culpable homicide applies to non-intentional killing where the *mens rea* is recklessness and intentional killing where a mitigating defence is available to the accused.

Hume deals with four categories of culpable homicide:

(1) An assault that results in death where there is no inference of intention or wicked recklessness.
(2) Death that results in the course of another unlawful act where the *mens rea* is recklessness.
(3) Where death occurs in the performance of a lawful act.
(4) Where the accused has the requisite *mens rea* for the crime of murder but a mitigating defence, *e.g.* the provocation or diminished

responsibility, serve to mitigate the responsibility of the accused. (i, 233–247)

Hume's four categories will be examined under the headings "voluntary" and "involuntary" culpable homicide. While the terms "voluntary", "involuntary" and Hume's four classifications are useful tools which we employ to examine culpable homicide it should be remembered that there is only one crime of culpable homicide. It is, therefore, not correct to refer to a criminal charge of voluntary culpable homicide or involuntary culpable homicide. In both of these instances the crime is culpable homicide.

Involuntary Culpable Homicide
This category of culpable homicide arises where death is caused unintentionally without the requisite degree of wicked recklessness or intention required for murder. It may take place in the course of a lawful or unlawful act and the *mens rea* is recklessness. This category of culpable homicide will be examined using three of Hume's (four) categories referred to above.

(1) An Assault that Results in Death. Where death results either in the course of an assault or as a result of an assault this will be charged at least as culpable homicide. The decision on whether the charge should be murder or culpable homicide is determined by the *mens rea*. The level of violence used in an assault will be very important in determining the *mens rea* and where severe violence has been used there is more chance that the *mens rea* of murder, wicked intention or wicked recklessness, will be inferred. Where death results from a minor assault and only recklessness can be inferred culpable homicide will be charged. In *Bird v. H.M. Advocate* (1952) the accused followed a woman whom he believed had taken his money. When the victim tried to get into a car the accused pulled her out. The fact that she had a weak heart and the threatening nature of the situation combined to cause her death. Bird was charged with culpable homicide. During the trial it was accepted that the accused would not have contemplated any risk of serious harm to his victim. In his charge to the jury the judge made it clear that the wrongful conduct required for a culpable homicide conviction could include no more than a mere threatening gesture. The jury returned a verdict of guilty.

(2) Death that Results in the Course of Another Unlawful Act. Where death occurs in the course of a crime other than assault this may also be charged as culpable homicide. Once again, where there is evidence of wicked intent or wicked recklessness a charge of murder would be appropriate. Culpable homicide will be charged where death results from a criminal act, the nature of which, or the degree of recklessness employed is such, that the risk of personal injury was reasonably forseeable. Not every criminal act which results in death will fulfil this requirement. Culpable homicide has been charged and the accused convicted in the following cases. Where death resulted from reckless fire-raising (*Mathieson v. H.M. Advocate* (1981)) and wilful fire-raising (*Sutherland v. H.M. Advocate* (1994)). In the unreported case of *Finnigan* (1958) (see Gordon, *Criminal Law*, para. 26.27) where the accused was convicted of culpable homicide when the death of an occupant of the building was the consequence of his stealing a gas meter by wrenching it from its supply pipe. In *Lord Advocate's Reference (No. 1 of 1994)* (1995) it was held that the crime of culpable homicide could result from the supply of a controlled drug to a recipient who died following ingestion. (The causation issues which arise in the last case are similar to those addressed by the court in *Khaliq v. H.M. Advocate* (1984), see Chapter 2.)

(3) Where Death Occurs in the Performance of a Lawful Act. A charge of culpable homicide arising from a recklessly performed lawful act requires recklessness and not merely carelessness or negligence on the part of the accused. Reported cases include road traffic offences, *e.g. Paton v. H.M. Advocate* (1935), however, similar cases now tend to be prosecuted under section 1 of the Road Traffic Act 1988 "causing death by dangerous driving". The reckless navigation of a boat (*Angus MacPherson and John Stewart* (1861)) and the reckless installation of a gas fire, where the failure to provide flues resulted in the death of two people from carbon monoxide poisoning (*Ross Fontana* (1990) unreported, see Jones and Christie, p. 218), both resulted in charges of culpable homicide.

Voluntary Culpable Homicide
The term voluntary culpable homicide is used to describe those situations where the accused is deemed to have killed intentionally or with wicked recklessness, *i.e.* have fulfilled the requirements for the crime of murder, but due to mitigating circumstances they are deemed to be guilty of culpable homicide. In these circumstances, the accused must have acted under provocation or diminished responsibility to have their actions classified as culpable homicide. The requirements of provocation and diminished responsibility are considered in Chapter 6.

As a matter of policy, certain types of conduct which in law amount to murder are charged as culpable homicide. These include suicide pacts where one of the parties survive and assisted euthanasia.

Attempted Culpable Homicide
There is no such crime as attempted culpable homicide because Scots law does not recognise reckless attempts. Where the conduct in question amounts to the crime of attempted murder but either provocation or diminished responsibility mitigate responsibility the appropriate verdict is one of assault.

EXTORTION

The *actus reus* of extortion is a threat accompanied by a demand and the *mens rea* is intention. There must be an actual threat, either express or implied, and where this is absent a demand on its own is not enough (*H.M. Advocate v. Donoghue* (1971)). The demand will generally be for money but it is not restricted to this. In *Rae v. Donnelly* (1982) the accused threatened to disclose alleged sexual impropriety unless the demand for resignation by one of the parties and the abandonment of a claim of unfair dismissal by the other was met. The crime of extortion requires that the demand is met. Where the demand is not met the accused may be convicted of attempted extortion (*Black v. Carmichael*; *Carmichael v. Black* (1992)). In *Black v. Carmichael*; *Carmichael v. Black*, Lord Justice-General Hope stated (at p. 717):

"In my opinion, it is extortion to seek to enforce a legitimate debt by means which the law regards as illegitimate, just as it is extortion to seek by such means to obtain money or some other advantage to which the accused has no right at all."

SEXUAL OFFENCES AGAINST THE PERSON

INDECENT ASSAULT

This crime is a form of aggravated assault and therefore has the same *mens rea* and *actus reus* as assault, namely, "evil intention" and "an attack against the person of another causing fear or alarm". The aggravation is lewdness or indecency. Indecent assault can be committed by a member of either sex against a member of either sex. Where the victim is of appropriate age, and non-violent sexual touching is consensual, then no crime has been committed as the accused lacks the necessary *mens rea* for the crime. Consensual acts are, therefore, not criminal. The crimes of indecent assault and rape are unique in that they are the only crimes where if the actions of the perpetrator are consensual they are deemed not to be criminal. This differs from, for example, assault or homicide where the consent of the victim does not negate the *mens rea* of the accused.

RAPE

Hume and writers who followed him regarded rape as a violent act committed against a resisting victim. The *actus reus* of rape is described as "the carnal knowledge of a female person by a male person obtained by force and overcoming her will." Some modern references to the crime of rape exclude the words "with force". Where there is no evidence of force, however, it may be difficult to show that intercourse was against the woman's will. The *mens rea* of the crime of rape is intention or recklessness. [Please see Appendix 2: Addendum on p. 99.]

Actus Reus

The *actus reus* requires the carnal knowledge of a female person by a male person. This is interpreted strictly to mean penetration of the vagina by the penis. There is no presumption in Scots law that a boy under the age of puberty cannot commit rape. Ejaculation is not necessary. This restricted definition means that penetration of other orifices or using other implements will not amount to rape but instead the less serious crime of indecent assault (*Barbour v. H.M. Advocate* (1982)). The definition also results in rape being a crime that can only be committed against women and the recognition of men as possible victims of the crime of rape in English law, by section 142 of the Criminal Justice and Public Order Act 1994, does not extend to Scotland. It is impossible for a woman to be charged as a principal offender with the crime of rape in Scotland but she could be charged art and part with a man.

The definition of rape makes no reference to the consent of the woman. The *actus reus* requires that the woman's will is overcome. Consequently, if a man has intercourse with a woman who is insensible, *e.g.* due to alcohol, drugs, or anaesthetics, he is not guilty of the crime of rape but clandestine injury, which is a serious form of indecent assault (*H.M. Advocate v. Grainger and Rae* (1932)). This is because the man did not require to overcome the woman's will. Case law includes situations where an accused had intercourse with a sleeping woman (*Charles Sweenie* (1858)) or an unconscious woman (*Sweeney v. X* (1982)). In these circumstances, to secure a conviction of rape, the Crown must prove that the woman had made her refusal to have intercourse known before becoming insensible. It is competent for a jury to return a verdict of guilty of indecent assault to a charge of rape (Criminal Law (Consolidation) (Scotland) Act 1995, s.14).

Where an accused makes a woman insensible for the purpose of having intercourse against her will then he can be convicted of the crime of rape (*H.M. Advocate v. Logan* (1935)). In these circumstances, the actions to make the woman insensible, *e.g.* administration of drink or drugs or knocking the woman unconscious, are deemed to be equivalent to force being used to overcome the woman's will. The Crown require to prove, however, that at the point the accused was overcoming the woman's will, *e.g.* with alcohol or drugs, that he was doing this with the intention of having intercourse with her. [Please see Appendix 2: Addendum on p. 99.]

Mens Rea

The *mens rea* of rape is either intention or recklessness. The crime of rape therefore requires that the accused intended to have intercourse against the woman's will or was reckless as to whether or not the woman was consenting to intercourse. Knowledge that a woman is not consenting to intercourse or indifference to the question of her consent, where she is not consenting, will fulfil the *mens rea* of rape.

The question which arises in most rape cases is not whether the accused was the person who had intercourse with the complainer but rather, was the intercourse which took place consensual or not. As the *mens rea* of rape requires that the accused intended to have intercourse against the woman's will, where the accused believes the woman is consenting to intercourse he is not deemed to have the requisite *mens rea*. In a rape trial the complainer's position is obviously that she did not consent to intercourse (as otherwise, her consent would mean that no crime was committed and therefore no trial would be necessary). In a trial, therefore, where an accused states that he believed the woman was consenting to intercourse, this is described as a mistaken belief. Prior to 1982, any such mistaken belief required to be both honest and reasonable before it would serve to negate the *mens rea*. The requirement of reasonableness meant that the claims of the accused would be assessed against what the reasonable person would have believed in the same circumstances. The decision of the High Court in *Meek v. H.M. Advocate* (1982) altered the test for mistaken belief in respect of the crime of rape.

In *Meek* three young men convicted of the rape of a 15-year-old girl appealed against their conviction on the ground that the trial judge had failed to direct the jury that they should be acquitted if they honestly believed that the girl had consented to intercourse. The trial judge had refused a motion by one of the defence counsel to direct the jury that the accused should be acquitted if they honestly believed that the woman was consenting even if there were not reasonable grounds for this belief. The trial judge did not give any direction on mistaken belief to the jury. The Appeal Court held that, where the facts raise an issue of mistaken belief in consent, it would be appropriate for the judge to direct the jury as counsel had requested. In the present case, however, the Court held that the issue of mistaken belief did not arise and instead the question for the jury was whether they believed the girl who said she had not consented or the accused who claimed that she had. The appeal was refused. The legal significance of this part of the judgment was not clear because it was *obiter dictum*. The legal position was, however, clarified in the subsequent case of *Jamieson v. H.M. Advocate* (1994).

In *Jamieson* the appellant had been convicted at trial of the rape of a woman. His defence was that the woman had consented to sexual intercourse or alternatively, even if she had not consented he had believed that she was consenting. He appealed against conviction on the grounds of a misdirection by the trial judge to the jury. The trial judge had directed the jury that a mistaken belief required to be both honest and reasonable. The Solicitor-General conceded, on behalf of the Crown, that there had been a misdirection. The appeal was successful and the conviction for rape was quashed. The opinion of the Court was delivered by Lord Justice-General Hope, he said (at p. 541):

"If a man has intercourse with a woman in the belief that she is consenting to this he cannot be guilty of rape. Now, the question whether the man believed that the woman consented is a question of fact. It is a question which the jury must decide, if it is raised, on the evidence. The grounds for his belief will be important, and if he has reasonable grounds for it the jury may find it easier to accept that he did honestly believe that the woman consented. But it will be open to the jury to accept his evidence on this point even if he cannot give grounds for it which they consider to be reasonable, and if they accept his evidence they must acquit him."

The Court also stated that where the man acted without thinking or was indifferent as to whether the woman was consenting, then that would not negate the *mens rea* of rape. This would fulfil the *mens rea* of recklessness.

In his report to the Appeal Court, the trial judge in *Jamieson* made reference to the fact that the decision in *Meek* was inconsistent with earlier authorities. In particular, those cases where a person has acted in self-defence in the mistaken belief that they are in danger of imminent death require that their mistaken belief be both honest and reasonable. The Court in *Jamieson* stated that this line of authority was unaffected by their decision. The Court distinguished rape because of the particular nature of the *mens rea* required to commit this crime. The decision in *Jamieson* confirmed that there are two forms of *mens rea* for the crime of rape, namely, intention and recklessness.

Marital Rape
Rape within marriage was not recognised as a crime in Scots law due to the statement by Hume that a husband cannot commit rape on his own wife, who has surrendered her person to him in that sort but that he could be an accessory to the crime of rape (i, 306). The recognition of rape within marriage began with *H.M. Advocate v. Duffy* (1983). It was not until *Stallard v. H.M. Advocate* (1989), however, that it was held to be relevant to charge a man with the rape of his wife with whom he was still co-habiting.

Fraud and Rape
The question of fraud and rape has arisen in only one reported Scottish case, *William Fraser* (1847). In that case the accused pretended to be the husband of the complainer and had intercourse with her. An objection to the relevancy of the charge of rape was sustained on the basis that the woman had consented to intercourse. The Sexual Offences (Scotland) Act 1976 has defined obtaining intercourse with a married woman by pretending to be her husband as rape in section 2(2).

The question of fraud remains a difficult question in Scots law. Where a woman freely participates in intercourse and does so in circumstances that amount to fraud (a false pretence leading to a practical result) this will not amount to rape. This is because the woman's will did not require to be overcome. This is problematic in situations where a woman is induced to have intercourse by the false statement by a man, for example, that he does not have a sexually transmitted disease or that he will pay her to have intercourse.

Capacity to Consent

The final issue that should be considered in respect of the crime of rape is capacity to consent. Intercourse with a girl below the age of 12 is rape even if the girl consents and her will is not overcome. The Mental Health (Scotland) Act 1984, s.106(1)(a), makes it an offence for a man to have unlawful, *i.e.* extra-marital intercourse, with a woman who is protected by section 106 due to her mental impairment. [Please see Appendix 2: Addendum on p. 99.]

OTHER SEXUAL OFFENCES

STATUTORY OFFENCE OF INTERCOURSE

Rape is a common law crime in Scotland, however, there are statutory provisions relating to intercourse with girls below the age of consent (16 years).

It is an offence to have or attempt to have intercourse with a girl under the age of 13. The crime is punishable by a maximum sentence of life imprisonment and an attempt at the crime by up to two years. The consent of the girl is no defence. This provision would normally only be used when the girl is between aged between 12 and 13, and if the girl is under 12 the crime will normally be charged as rape (Criminal Law (Consolidation) (Scotland) Act 1995, s.5).

It is an offence to have intercourse with a girl between the ages of 13 and 16. It is a defence if the man was under 24, had no similar previous convictions and had reasonable cause to believe the girl was over 16 (Criminal Law (Consolidation) (Scotland) Act 1995, s.5(5)).

CLANDESTINE INJURY

As noted above, this common law offence arises where the accused has had intercourse with a woman who is temporarily unable to give or refuse consent, and consequently there is no element of force or overcoming of will (*Charles Sweenie* (1858) and *X v. Sweeney* (1982)).

LEWD PRACTICES

It is a common law offence to behave in a lewd, indecent and libidinous manner towards or in the presence of children under the age of puberty (girls aged 12 and boys aged 14). There is no defence of consent to this crime. The *mens rea* is knowingly or intentionally committing the act against the child in question. The act can involve direct contact with the child or indecent displays in the presence of a child. Under section 5 of the Criminal Law (Consolidation) (Scotland) Act 1995 it is a separate statutory offence to commit lewd practices towards a girl aged between 12 and 16.

INCEST

The current law in this area was consolidated by the Incest and Related Offences (Scotland) Act 1986. The relevant provisions are now found in the Criminal Law (Consolidation) (Scotland) Act 1995 (ss.1–4). This Act makes it an offence for any male or female to have sexual intercourse with a person of the opposite sex who falls within the forbidden degrees of relationship. Sexual intercourse is not defined in this legislation but it is presumed to mean penetration of the vagina by the penis. The forbidden degrees of relationship reflect the forbidden degrees of marriage. This legislation also introduces a new offence of intercourse by a person in a position of trust with a child under the age of 16.

Both parties are liable to prosecution under these statutory provisions. The defences to an incest charge are ignorance to the relationship between the parties, that intercourse was not consensual and that the parties were married at the time, the marriage having been entered into outwith Scotland and recognised as valid.

SHAMELESS INDECENCY

The scope of the crime of shameless indecency is very wide and has been held to apply to a broad range of acts. In *Watt v. Annan* (1978) the accused was charged with shameless indecency as a consequence of showing a pornographic film to members of a private club. In *Usai v. Russell* (2000) the accused was charged with shameless indecency when he exposed himself at the window of a lit room to women in neighbouring properties.

HOMOSEXUAL OFFENCES

Intercourse involving anal penetration between two males that is non-consensual is charged as sodomy. Where the act is consensual both parties are guilty at common law, but would not be prosecuted if they fall within the provisions of section 1(3) of the Sexual Offences (Amendment) Act 2000. This legislation provides that homosexual intercourse between consenting males over the age of 16 and in private is not an offence. "Private" excludes situations where more than two persons are present. All other homosexual behaviour, whether intercourse or "gross indecency" remains a crime at common law. Until the Criminal Justice and Public Order Act 1994, the age of "consent" for homosexuals was 21, and this was reduced to 18 by section 13 of the Criminal Law (Consolidation) (Scotland) Act 1995, and is now 16.

READING

P. W. Ferguson, *Crimes Against the Person* (2nd ed., Butterworths, Edinburgh, 1998), Chaps 1–4, 7 and 8.

C. Gane, *Sexual Offences* (Butterworths, Edinburgh, 1992).

C. Gane, C. Stoddart and J. Chalmers, *A Casebook on Scottish Criminal Law* (3rd ed., W. Green & Son, Edinburgh, 2001), Chaps 8–10 and pp. 490–493.

G. H. Gordon, *Criminal Law* (3rd ed., M. Christie (ed.), W. Green & Son, Edinburgh, 2001), Vol. II.

T. Jones and M. Christie, *Criminal Law* (2nd ed., W. Green & Son, Edinburgh, 1996), Chap. 9.

R. McCall Smith and D. Sheldon, *Scots Criminal Law* (Butterworths, Edinburgh, 1997), Chaps 9–11.

----

4. CRIMES OF DISHONESTY AND AGAINST PROPERTY

THEFT

The definition of the law of theft has changed over time. The definition given by Hume was "the felonious taking and carrying away of the property of another, for profit". The crime was strictly defined and required the actual taking of property, the intention to permanently deprive the owner and that the taking must be for profit. This strict definition was probably due to theft being a capital offence at the time. The modern definition of theft can be described as having an *actus reus* of appropriation, which incorporates theft achieved by taking or finding, and the *mens rea* is no longer restricted to an intention permanently to deprive the owner of their property. The requirement "for lucre", *i.e.* profit, no longer applies to theft and it is the owner's loss rather than the other's gain which is important (*Black v. Carmichael; Carmichael v. Black* (1992)). The current definition of theft can be stated as:

> *The appropriation of the goods or property of another without the consent of the owner and with the intent to deprive them of that property.*

The modern law of theft continues to develop with questions over what can be stolen, *e.g.* computer data; how something can be stolen, *e.g.* depriving the owner of the use of their property; and, what form an intention to deprive should take, *e.g.* permanent, indefinite, or temporary. The current definition of theft can be broken into the following elements:

(1) the appropriation;

(2) of the property of another which is capable of being stolen;

(3) without the consent of the owner; and

(4)   with the intention to deprive the owner of that property.

The first three of these requirements relate to the *actus reus* and the fourth to the *mens rea*.

Actus Reus of Theft

(1) Appropriation

Appropriation is now assumed to cover theft by taking, theft by finding and also where goods already in possession are appropriated. Hume's definition of theft did not include those circumstances where a person found goods and retained them or where a person who is in possession of goods, with the consent of the owner, appropriates them for his own use. Appropriation includes: where goods are taken from the owner without their consent (*Barr v. O'Brien* (1991)); where goods given for one purpose are used for another (*Dewar v. H.M. Advocate* (1945)); where the owner is prevented from using his goods (*Black v. Carmichael*; *Carmichael v. Black* (1992)); and, where goods found are appropriated for the owner's own use (*John Smith* (1838); *MacMillan v. Lowe* (1991)).

In addition to the common law provisions which recognise theft by finding, there are statutory provisions. The Civic Government (Scotland) Act 1982, ss.67–75, provides that it is an offence if the finder of property fails to take reasonable care of it and report the finding to the police or the owner/occupier of the premises where the property was found. If a person finding property contravenes this provision they will not only have breached the statute but their actions will allow the *mens rea* of theft, namely, intention, to be inferred from their actions.

Where theft is of goods already in the possession of the thief the crime is committed at the point the custodier forms the intention to deprive the owner of their goods by appropriating them. Evidence of this intention is, of course, necessary and may be more difficult to infer than in the case of theft by taking. As a result, it is almost impossible in such cases to differentiate the *actus reus* and *mens rea* of theft. There is no act of taking and the thief is authorised to possess and, in some cases, to carry out certain acts involving the property. Therefore, the conduct of the accused must be examined to infer at which point the intention to appropriate the goods was formed.

In *Dewar* the accused, a manager of a crematorium, was convicted of the theft of two coffins and the lids of a large number of other coffins. In a statement to the police Dewar admitted the practice of retaining the coffins and said that this was the general practice throughout the crematorium movement. The appropriation of the property was fulfilled at the point Dewar retained the coffins and lids rather than incinerating them. In *Carmichael*, the accused was charged with the crime of extortion and, alternatively, the theft of two cars. The accused had wheel clamped the cars and placed a notice on the windscreen stating that the clamp would be removed upon payment of a fine. The cars were parked in a private car park without permission. In this case the property was appropriated at the point the wheel was clamped, thereby depriving the owner's of the use of their property.

Dewar may suggest that appropriation requires that the accused has assumed the full rights of the owner in respect of the appropriated property. However, *Carmichael* illustrates that it is not necessary for either the owner of the goods to have given over their full rights in the property nor for the accused to have assumed the full rights of the owner.

Theft by appropriation is fully explained in *Black v. Carmichael*; *Carmichael v. Black* (1992) (at pp. 719–720), where the Lord Justice-General Hope said:

"[T]he essential feature of the physical act necessary to constitute theft is the appropriation, by which control and possession of the thing is taken from its owner or custodier. In principle, therefore, the removal of the thing does not seem to be necessary, if the effect of the act which is done to it is its appropriation by the accused ... It seems to me that the act of depriving the motorist of the use of his motor-car by detaining it against his will can accurately be described as stealing something from him and that, on this basis, the facts libelled are sufficient to constitute a charge of theft. The accused are said to have deliberately placed a wheel clamp on a wheel of a vehicle which they found in the car park, in order to detain it there and keep it under their control against the will of the motorist. There is no suggestion that it was intended by the motorist that they (the accused) should have control over the car for any purpose, or that by parking the vehicle in the car park he (the motorist) intended that anyone else should have control over it. And the physical element of appropriation is clearly present, in my opinion, since the purpose and effect of the wheel clamp was to immobilise the vehicle and to deprive the motorist of his possession and use of it as [a] motor car."

(2) Property of Another Capable of Being Stolen

Before property can be stolen it requires to be publicly or privately owned by another person, capable of being moved and must be corporeal. In general, people cannot steal their own property. The possible exception to this would be that the directors of a company could be held liable for stealing from the company (*Sandlan v. H.M. Advocate* (1983)). Remember, however, that the company is a separate legal entity so it is not the same as stealing your own property.

Property Publicly or Privately Owned by Another Person. If a person takes property in the mistaken belief that it is his or her own, a question would arise as to whether they have the requisite intention to deprive the owner of the property. If these actions result in a charge of theft it is open to an accused to use erroneous claim of right as a defence. The test applied in these circumstances is an objective one, *i.e.*

was the accused's belief both honest and reasonable. It is not enough that the accused believes his actions are not criminal, rather, there must be an erroneous claim of right.

In *Dewar* the accused was convicted of the theft of two coffins and the lids of a large number of other coffins. In a statement to the police Dewar admitted the practice of retaining the coffins and said that this was the general practice throughout the crematorium movement. Dewar's position was that upon delivery to the crematorium the coffins and lids were completely under his jurisdiction for disposal. Evidence at the trial demonstrated that this was not the common practice. At trial, the jury were directed on the law relating to erroneous claims of right. The Lord Justice-Clerk Cooper directed the jury (at pp. 7–8):

"[To consider] not only the fact that the explanation offered by Dewar was false, and is now admitted to be false, but you will also consider whether he had any colourable ground for holding such a view, or whether the statements made by him to the police ... and other people ... with regard to the practice of the crematorium movement were made recklessly without any justification for belief in their accuracy."

The jury was, therefore, directed to consider whether Dewar's belief was both honest and reasonable. On appeal, Lord Justice-General Normand stated (at p. 11):

"It is contrary to the appellant's own evidence that the coffins were completely under his jurisdiction for disposal ... His evidence is a plain assertion of his unlimited right of property in a thing which he knew was sent to him under contract for the purpose of destruction ... Accordingly, in my opinion, there was misappropriation of property which he knew was sent to him merely for destruction by a prescribed method."

Whilst Lord Justice-General Normand made it clear that in his opinion the trial judge did not require to direct the jury on Dewar's erroneous claim of right, some commentators, *e.g.* Jones and Christie, 1996, p. 165, have not accepted this position. If Dewar honestly believed that he could dispose of the coffins and lids as he pleased, *i.e.* he was confused as regards the law of property, would he have the requisite *mens rea* of intention for the crime of theft? Before a belief could negate *mens rea* it would be tested objectively and requires to be reasonable as well as honest. (The approach in the law of rape (*Meek* (1982) and *Jamieson* (1994)) where an honest belief, even if unreasonable, negates *mens rea* does not apply to other crimes.) The jury in *Dewar* clearly did not accept that his mistaken belief was both honest and reasonable.

Things that are not owned are *res nullius*, and cannot be stolen. Any property, which is abandoned, is deemed to belong to the Crown. Wild animals are not owned and therefore cannot be stolen, but if they are brought into ownership, *e.g.* captured and enclosed, they may thereafter be stolen. In *Valentine v. Kennedy* (1985) trout which had been purchased from a fish farm were put in an enclosure. The trout escaped from this and were swimming in a burn when the accused and his friends began poaching and caught some fish. The accused were discovered and charged with theft. The trout which had been caught were identified as rainbow trout that had been farmed at the fish farm. The sheriff held that they were still owned, they were capable of being stolen and the accused were convicted of theft.

In *Kane v. Friel* (1997) the appellant had been convicted of theft by finding metal piping and a sink and appealed to the High Court. The police did not see the appellant and his brother taking the property but instead met them, already in possession of the property, crossing waste ground. They told the police they had found the goods and they were going to sell them. At trial, the justice held that they had found the property and appropriated it and also that this property had not been reported as stolen. On appeal, Lord Justice-General Rodger noted (at pp. 208–209) that while at common law most abandoned property belongs to the Crown, the advocate–depute did not attempt to find on that "technical doctrine" nor the duties under the Civic Government (Scotland) Act 1982 (s.67), to take care of and deliver property which is found to a police constable or the owner/occupier of the land upon which it is found. In terms of the *mens rea* of theft, the advocate-depute had accepted that the Crown required to prove that the accused must have intended to appropriate the items dishonestly. Lord Justice-General Rodger concluded (at p. 210) that the Crown had not proved anything about the circumstances in which the piping or sink were found; there was nothing which would give the justice a basis for inferring that the appellant must have known that the items were property which someone intended to retain; and, that it was relevant that the items had not been reported stolen. Allowing the appeal he stated:

> "In that situation we are satisfied that there was no sufficient basis on which the justice could infer that the appellant had the necessary dishonest intention to appropriate the copper and the sink. We refer to Mackenzie *v. Maclean* [1981], where, in unusual circumstances, the sheriff acquitted the accused on the ground that the Crown had not proved the necessary dishonesty for theft."

Moveable Corporeal Property. Generally, the rule is that something must be moveable (corporeal property) before it can be stolen. Consequently, land cannot be stolen but things that are grown on the land may be stolen. Money and documents which contain the person's right to a thing, *e.g.* share certificates, can be stolen. On the basis of taking the document that represents the incorporeal property, *e.g.* the share certificate, the thief cannot be charged with the theft of the actual shares. Air, water, gas and electricity can be stolen and charges of theft have resulted from, *e.g.* the bypassing of an electricity meter.

Property that is not moveable is known as incorporeal property. Incorporeal property, *e.g.* a person's right to something, cannot be stolen. Problems arise over the theft of information, *e.g.* computer databases. In *Grant v. Allan* (1987) the court held that the accused,

making copies of computer print-outs belonging to his employers, may
have breached an express or implied obligation to keep material
confidential but that it did not amount to criminal conduct.

Human beings cannot be stolen but can be kidnapped, which is a
distinct and separate crime. The exception to this rule relates to pre-
pubescent children. There is the Scots common law crime of child
stealing, which is called plagium. This crime can be committed by
anyone including a parent who removes their own child, *e.g.* in custody
disputes. Recent cases include *Downie v. H.M. Advocate* (1984) and
Hamilton v. Mooney (1990). In *Downie* the accused was the biological
father of a child but was neither married to the child's mother not did he
have custody of the child. The jury were charged that in the absence of a
custody decree the father of an illegitimate child had no rights to the
child and could in theory be convicted of stealing it. If the remains of
human beings are stolen from a grave this does not amount to the crime
of theft but is the special crime of violation of sepulchres.

(3) Without the Consent of the Owner

If the owner agreed to the transfer of goods to the accused, even if the
consent is obtained by fraud, then so long as the consent of the owner is
clear and is to the permanent appropriation of the goods the crime of
theft has not been committed. The actions of the accused may, however,
result in another charge, most commonly, fraud. Where an accused has a
mistaken belief that the owner consented to the removal of goods, then
so long as this belief is both honest and reasonable (an objective test),
she will lack the necessary *mens rea* for the crime of theft.

Mens Rea of Theft

(4) Intention to Deprive the Owner of their Property

The *mens rea* of intention in the crime of theft will be inferred from the
facts of the case. Until relatively recently, the *mens rea* of theft was
understood to be an intention to deprive permanently an owner of their
property. As a consequence, any temporary deprivation was not
regarded as theft but the lesser crime of clandestinely taking and using
the property of another, *e.g. Strathern v. Seaforth* (1926). Recent case
law has introduced a more flexible approach to the *mens rea* of theft but
there is a lack of consistency in these decisions. These decisions are
discussed under the following headings: intention permanently to
deprive; intention to deprive for a nefarious purpose; intention to
deprive indefinitely and intention to deprive temporarily.

Intention Permanently to Deprive. Permanent deprivation refers to
where the accused intends to deprive the owner of their property
on a permanent basis. The earliest challenge to the accepted rule that
permanent deprivation is necessary for the crime of theft is found in
Kivlin v. Milne (1979). In this case the accused was convicted of theft

when they took a car without the permission of the owner and left it in a place where the owner was unlikely to find it. No formal opinion was issued but in dismissing the appeal their Lordships said (at p. 2):

"[T]he learned Sheriff ... was entitled to draw the inference that the appellant had the intention permanently to deprive the owner of the motor car of the possession thereof, in that he undoubtedly took possession of it without authority and left the car on each occasion in a place where the owner, by reason of his own investigations, was not liable to discover it."

In this case, the *mens rea* of theft is still referred to as an intention to permanently deprive the owner of their property. There is, however, some relaxation of the interpretation of permanent and, as a result, the actions of the accused will be held to amount to a permanent deprivation where an owner cannot, on his own investigations, find his car.

Intention to Deprive for a Nefarious Purpose. This form of *mens rea* has been suggested in cases where the accused withholds property of another until a demand is met. In all of the reported cases the demand has been for money. In *Milne v. Tudhope* (1981) two accused were convicted of the theft of articles they removed from a cottage without the consent of the owner. The accused had been contracted to carry out work on the cottage and when the owner refused to pay additional monies for remedial work that required to be done, the accused removed radiators, a boiler, etc., which the owner had paid for. On appeal, the High Court held that (at p. 55): "a clandestine taking aimed at achieving a nefarious purpose, constitutes theft, even if the taker intends all along to return the thing taken when the purpose has been achieved." The Court did stress that it was only in certain exceptional circumstances that an intention to deprive temporarily would suffice.

The approach in *Milne* was followed in *Kidston v. Annan* (1984) which involved the accused being convicted of theft as a result of having retained a television set until repairs had been paid for. The owner of the television claimed that he had requested a quote and had not instructed any repairs. In both cases the owner's property was being retained until money was paid to the accused. In *Kidston*, the High Court referred to this as holding property to ransom. Such actions have been held to amount to a "nefarious purpose", but this term has also been used in the case *Sandlan v. H.M. Advocate* (1983) which did not involve property being held to ransom. In *Sandlan*, property was removed temporarily, the prosecution claimed, to falsely obtain insurance money. In this case the appellant was a director of the company that the articles were taken from. The second accused, King, gave evidence in his defence, that the goods were only to be removed for a short period so that pilfering by Sandlan would be disguised during stocktaking. Lord Stewart directed the jury that if they accepted King's explanation then the actions of the accused amounted to a nefarious purpose.

This opinion suggests that the court view an intention to deprive for a nefarious purpose necessary before theft can arise from temporary deprivation of property. Later authorities, *e.g. Black v. Carmichael; Carmichael v. Black* (1992), have said that there is no requirement for a "nefarious purpose" even when appropriation is temporary.

Intention to Deprive Indefinitely. This further development in the *mens rea* of theft arose in *Fowler v. O'Brien* (1994). The appellant was convicted of theft at the district court. He had requested a shot of the complainer's bike and when the latter refused he took the bicycle. The appellant claimed that he told the complainer that he would leave the bicycle at the swimming pool. It is not clear if this was accepted by the justice of the peace but there was evidence that the complainer searched for his bike, including around the swimming pool, and did not recover it for several days. The High Court stated that the facts did not entitle the justice to conclude that there was an intention to permanently or temporarily deprive the owner of their property. The Court held that (at p. 115):

> "[It] would be more accurate to say that the owner was indefinitely deprived of their property, since it was not made clear to him whether, and if so, when it would ever be returned to him. In these circumstances there was no need for any clandestine or nefarious purpose to be established. There was no need for any exceptional circumstances. The question is simply whether the necessary criminal intention was present for the taking away of the bicycle to amount to theft. We are persuaded, in the light of the findings, that the justice was entitled to reach the view and to regard this as an act of stealing of the bicycle."

Intention to Deprive Temporarily. In *Black v. Carmichael*; *Carmichael v. Black* (1992) the Court held that an intention to deprive the owner of their property temporarily will suffice for the crime of theft. Unlike earlier decisions, they do not make reference to temporary deprivation amounting to permanent deprivation (*Kivlin*) nor any requirement for a nefarious purpose to be proven (*Milne, Kidston*). The opinions delivered in this case stress that it is the owner's loss and not the other's gain which is important in relation to the crime of theft.

AGGRAVATED THEFT

The crime of theft can be aggravated by a number of factors that relate to forcing entry to premises so that a theft can be committed. The aggravations are examined below.

THEFT BY OPENING LOCKFAST PLACES

This aggravation involves overcoming the security of anything other than a building. The opening of a lockfast place must precede and be for the purpose of the theft. Examples would include the opening of a parked car, see *McLeod v. Mason* (1981). It is unnecessary to specify whether the thief intended to steal the car or something within the car. It is necessary that the car was secure.

THEFT BY HOUSEBREAKING

This aggravation applies when the security of any type of shut and fast roofed building is overcome. The housebreaking must precede the theft. Consequently, a thief who hides in a shop and after it is secured takes items and breaks out of the shop has not committed an aggravated theft. In *Lafferty v. Wilson* (1990) the accused was convicted of housebreaking. This resulted from breaking into an unoccupied flat in November 1988. Before July 1988 this flat had been the subject of a number of housebreakings. On appeal, the conviction was quashed as it could not be proven first, that the flat was secure prior to the accused gaining entry and second, that the accused had overcome the security of the building.

HOUSEBREAKING WITH INTENT TO STEAL

This aggravation is charged when the accused unsuccessfully attempts the crime of theft by housebreaking (*Burns v. Allan* (1987)).

ROBBERY

Where theft is accomplished by personal violence or intimidation, it is the crime of robbery. As theft is an essential element of robbery, the law relating to theft, namely, the *mens rea* and the *actus reus* apply equally to robbery. The caveat to this is that robbery will always involve taking rather than appropriation of goods already in the possession of the accused. This is because robbery requires the violent removal of goods from the victim. The goods do not need to belong to the victim, it is enough if the victim is acting as a custodian. In *Flynn v. H.M. Advocate* (1995) the appellant and another man were charged with assault and robbery. The jury returned a verdict of not proven in respect of the assault charge subject to a deletion of "seize him by the throat, repeatedly punch him on the face whereby he fell to the ground" and a verdict of guilty of robbery. This conviction was appealed on the ground that a conviction of robbery was perverse where all reference to violence had been deleted. The Court held that where an indictment libels a charge of robbery and details the violence used, the jury are not entitled to convict of robbery where they have deleted any reference to the accused being responsible for any violence either on his own or while acting art and part. The Court observed that it would be competent to bring a charge of robbery without specifying the violence used.

Any degree of violence or intimidation is sufficient so long as it is for the purpose of stealing the property (*MacKay v. H.M. Advocate* (1997)). This violence does not need to involve wounding or beating. In

Cromar v. H.M. Advocate (1987) the accused came up behind the complainer and pulled at a bag of money he was holding until the handle snapped. The accused appealed against his conviction of robbery on the basis that he should only have been charged with theft as he only pulled the bag once. The Court held that there was sufficient evidence to entitle the jury to reach the conclusion that theft had been accomplished by personal violence and that, therefore, the crime was robbery.

Intimidation may consist of any threat of immediate injury that induces the victim to hand over the property. Violence that occurs after seizing property does not amount to robbery and in these circumstances the appropriate charges are assault and theft.

EMBEZZLEMENT

The crime of embezzlement involves a dishonest failure to account for goods entrusted to the accused. The accused will not only have had possession of the goods but also the power to undertake transactions as if the property was his own. The *actus reus* requires an unauthorised act on the part of the accused and the *mens rea* is a dishonest and felonious intent to appropriate the property of another. Evidence of dishonesty is necessary (*Allenby v. H.M. Advocate* (1938)).

The *mens rea* and *actus reus* of theft and embezzlement are, therefore, very similar, namely, intention and appropriation. Differences between the two crimes are more difficult to identify. One such difference is that whilst incorporeal property cannot be stolen it can be embezzled (*Guild v. Lees* (1994)). An interesting difference is that professional people who appropriate goods in their trust embezzle whereas non-professional people steal (*Edgar v. MacKay* (1926)). The ability to distinguish between the two crimes is now of less importance, as it is competent to return a conviction of theft on a charge of embezzlement and vice versa (Criminal Procedure (Scotland) Act 1995, Sched. 3).

FRAUD

Fraud was defined by MacDonald as the "bringing about of any practical result by false pretences" (MacDonald, 52).

The *actus reus* of fraud requires a false pretence, a practical result and a causal link between the false pretence and the practical result. The *mens rea* requires that the accused acted intentionally with the knowledge that the pretence was false.

The false pretence can be express or implied and may result from either positive actions or a failure to do something. An express action has been held to include where the accused misrepresents the value of work done to property (*H.M. Advocate v. McAllister* (1996)) and an implied action, where animals being displayed at a prize show were made more attractive (*James Paton* (1858)). A failure to disclose relevant information to the rating authorities was held to be sufficient for the *actus reus* of fraud in *Strathern v. Fogal* (1922). The result of the false pretence will be dependent on the type of pretence. The important factor is that the victim must have acted in a way that they would not otherwise have done without the false pretence.

The *mens rea* of fraud necessitates that the accused knew that the pretence was false and intended to deceive the other party. Recklessness is not recognised as sufficient for the *mens rea* of fraud. In *Mackenzie v. Skeen* (1971) the accused was extremely careless when he weighed offal that was to be sold to pet food manufacturers. In the absence of an intention to deceive either his employer or the owner of the pet food company he was acquitted of fraud.

Case law has demonstrated that a charge of fraud can be the result where the accused makes a false representation relating to a future intention. In *Richards v. H.M. Advocate* (1971) the appellant was convicted of fraud when he induced Edinburgh Corporation to sell property to his nominee under the false pretence that it was to be used as a private residence. He appealed on the grounds, *inter alia*, that the misrepresentation did not relate to a present but future intention. The Appeal Court refused the appeal. In cases such as *Richards* it would be open to an accused to change his mind. This decision underlines that it is the accused's present intention as to her future actions which is relevant. This is of relevance in relation to financial transactions involving cheques, etc. Where a cheque is written and the individual neither has funds in their bank account nor do they intend to lodge funds in their bank account prior to the cheque being presented, they have committed the crime of fraud. This person has the necessary intention as to her future actions to deceive. This differs from the person who writes a cheque knowing that they do not have sufficient funds but who intends to lodge additional funds prior to the cheque being presented. If the funds are lodged of course the situation would never come to light, but it is important that this individual does not at the time of writing the cheque have the necessary intention to commit the crime of fraud.

RESET

Hume defined reset as "the receiving and keeping of stolen goods, knowing them to be such, and with an intention to conceal and withhold them from the owner" (i, 113). Whilst reset was originally limited to the retention of those goods obtained by theft or robbery, this has now been extended to include goods obtained by fraud, embezzlement and breach of trust (Criminal Law (Consolidation) (Scotland) Act 1995, s.51). The *actus reus* of reset is the retention of goods obtained dishonestly and the *mens rea* is knowledge of the origin of the goods and the intention to withhold the property from the true owner. It is not possible to be convicted of the theft and reset of the same property, however, it is competent to return a verdict of guilty of reset on a charge of theft. A conviction of theft cannot, however, be returned on a charge of reset probably because the former is a more serious crime.

Actus Reus

Hume and subsequent case law stated that the _actus reus_ of reset required that the accused take possession of the goods. Any period of possession, however slight, is sufficient (_Robert Finlay_ (1826)). The crime is committed at the point of receipt of the goods. It is not necessary for the accused to intend to retain the goods permanently. The actual goods must be retained and retention of the proceeds from the sale of the goods does not amount to reset. Retention can occur either from purchasing the goods or retaining them on behalf of a third party on a gratuitous basis. It is not necessary for the accused to receive the goods directly from the thief. Where stolen property has been passed amongst a number of individuals it may be more difficult to prove the requisite _mens rea_ for each to be found guilty of reset.

Contrary to the views of Hume and others, MacDonald suggests that the crime of reset can be committed where an accused is "privy to the retaining of property that has been dishonestly come by" (p. 67). This removes the necessity that the accused has taken possession of the goods. In _H.M. Advocate v. Browne_ (1903), Lord Justice-Clerk Kinsburgh (MacDonald) directed a jury that (p. 26):

"If a man steals a bundle of notes out of a man's pocket and after that informs another man that he has got these notes ... or if the man saw him stealing them and knew they were stolen, then if the other man connived at it remaining in the possession of the thief or being out in any place for safe custody, such as hiding in a cupboard, he is guilty of receiving feloniously even although he never puts his fingers on the notes at all."

It is not clear from the reported cases what is required for connivance, however, _Browne_ suggests that it may be inferred from inactivity on the part of the accused. While this has been followed in some cases, _e.g. McNeil v. H.M. Advocate_ (1968), it has been questioned in others. In _Clark v. H.M. Advocate_ (1965) Lord Justice-Clerk Grant held that the sheriff's direction that connivance could be inferred from mere inactivity on the part of the accused was incorrect. In _Hipson v. Tudhope_ (1983) Lord Justice-Clerk Wheatley said (at p. 660):

"The only point at issue is whether there was evidence which warranted the sheriff arriving at the decision ... that the appellant was privy to the retention of the stolen car so as to constitute the crime of reset ... All the appellant said when he was cautioned and charged was simply 'not guilty'. In that situation ... I am of [the] opinion that the situation clearly falls into the category that was recognised in _Clark v. H.M. Advocate_ ... as being a situation where an inference of guilty knowledge could not be gathered from the mere silence of the accused."

Mens Rea

The *mens rea* of reset is knowledge that the goods have been obtained dishonestly and an intention to deprive the owner of the goods. Knowledge of the source of goods can be difficult to establish. It is not enough for an accused to say that they did not appreciate the source of goods and where an accused "wilfully blinds himself" to the origin of goods this will not act as a defence to a charge of reset (*Latta v. Herron* (1967)). If an accused honestly and reasonably believes that goods are from an honest source she will lack the requisite *mens rea* for the crime of reset.

An evidential rule that assists in proving the *mens rea* of both reset and theft is the doctrine of recent possession. The doctrine is that an inference of guilt can be drawn from an accused being in possession of recently stolen property in *criminative* circumstances (*Davidson v. Brown* (1990)). The *mens rea* of reset can also be inferred from the accused's account of how she came to be in possession of goods. If an accused provides an awkward explanation of how she came to be in possession of stolen goods the jury are entitled to infer from this that the accused had the knowledge necessary for the crime of reset (*Forbes v. H.M. Advocate* (1995)).

Wife's Privilege

Traditionally in Scots law a wife could not be convicted of reset of property stolen by her husband. This approach was varied in the case *Smith v. Watson* (1982) where a wife was convicted of the reset of money that her husband had stolen. The money was posted through her letterbox while her husband was in prison having already been convicted of the robbery from which the money was the proceeds. The Court held that the money was not being retained to protect or shield the husband but for his subsequent use on his release from prison. In these circumstances, the wife's privilege was held not to apply.

UTTERING AS GENUINE

Forgery is not a crime at common law unless the forgery is "uttered", *i.e.* presented to a third party as genuine. It is necessary that the perpetrator knows that the document is forged and intends that the other party should be deceived by it. A practical result is not necessary (see Hume, i, 148–149 and *Burke v. MacPhail* (1984)).

OFFENCES AGAINST PROPERTY

In this section the crimes of malicious mischief, vandalism and fire-raising will be considered.

MALICIOUS MISCHIEF

Malicious mischief is the intentional or reckless damage of property without the owner's consent. The property must belong to another person. Hume's definition of this crime required physical damage to the property and some element of civil disturbance. However, the current law no longer requires any civil disturbance (*Ward v. Robertson* (1938)), and the definition of damage to property has been extended to include patrimonial loss caused by the actions of the accused (*H.M. Advocate v. Wilson* (1984)).

In *Wilson* the accused was charged with malicious mischief when he pressed the emergency button of a turbine at a power station which resulted in electricity to the value of £147,000 having to be replaced from other sources. The accused was acquitted at trial and the Crown appealed to the High Court. In his report to the High Court the sheriff stated (at p. 117):

"My reason for holding the indictment irrelevant ... is that hitherto the crime of malicious mischief has necessarily involved some physical damage or injury to property ... It is not libelled that any physical damage was done to the generator. It may be desirable that the law should regard as criminal any wilful or reckless act which causes financial loss, but hitherto that has not been understood by the law."

The Lord Justice-Clerk (Lord Wheatley, at p. 119), held that the crime of malicious mischief:

"[H]as to be a deliberate and malicious act to damage another's property, or to interfere with it to the detriment of the owner or lawful possessor ... This leaves for consideration only the question whether what resulted from this initial act was 'damage' or 'patrimonial loss' ... In my opinion, the occurrence has to be looked at as a whole. If the malicious intention improperly to stop the production of electricity is established, and the achievement of that had the effect of rendering inoperative a machine which should have been operating productively and profitably, then in my view that is just as much damage to the employer's property as would be the case in any of the more physical acts of sabotage."

His Lordship concluded that the crime libelled falls within Hume's definition of malicious mischief.

Lord McDonald agreed with Lord Wheatley, however, Lord Stewart dissented stating (at p. 122):

"This is not in my view, merely a case where the modus of an established crime may change with changing circumstances. Rather is it a case where an essential constituent of the crime is seen to be missing from the libel. I do not consider that the failure of a machine to operate through being switched off can be equated to the failure of a machine to be able to operate through being destroyed or damaged ... I consider that actual destruction or damage is an essential of the crime."

The approach in *Wilson* has been confirmed in *Bett v. Hamilton* (1997), however, a limit has been placed on what qualifies as patrimonial loss. In *Bett* the accused was convicted of malicious mischief when he changed the angle of a bank security camera. It was suggested that the costs of running the security camera were wasted and that there was an increased risk of housebreaking, theft or vandalism. Lord Sutherland delivered the opinion of the Court, at pp. 623–624:

> "What is required in such a charge [malicious mischief] is that there should be a wilful intent to cause injury to the owner or possessor of the property. This injury may either be in the form of physical damage or in the form of patrimonial loss. We do not consider that the matters referred to by the advocate-depute properly constitute patrimonial loss. The running costs of the camera would have been incurred in any event, even if it had been pointing in the right direction, and accordingly what has been lost to the bank is such benefit as they may have obtained from the fact that the camera was pointing in the correct direction ... The bank on these averments suffered no financial loss whatsoever and therefore there is no patrimonial loss."

Where an accused damages the property of another in the belief that he is legally justified this will not act as a defence (*Clark v. Syme* (1957)). This applies even where the accused acts on the basis of vindication of rights, *i.e.* that an individual may damage another person's property, in order to protect their own property rights.

VANDALISM

Vandalism is the statutory equivalent to malicious mischief. The offence was created in 1980 and the current law is contained within section 52 of the Criminal Law (Consolidation) (Scotland) Act 1995. This section states that "any person who, without reasonable excuse, wilfully or recklessly destroys or damages any property belonging to another shall be guilty of the offence of vandalism". The *mens rea* required is either intention or recklessness. One difference between vandalism and malicious mischief is that the former requires that the damage or destruction be done "without reasonable excuse". Where an accused presents a "reasonable excuse" the onus is on the prosecution to prove that the excuse is not reasonable (*MacDouga
l v. Yuk-Sun Ho* (1985)).

FIRE-RAISING

The crime of fire-raising is a serious form of malicious mischief. Traditionally this was a capital offence where the property burned was houses, corn, coal heughs, woods and under-woods (Hume, i, 31). Fire-raising involves the intentional or reckless damaging or destroying of corporeal property belonging to another without his consent or permission. The crime of fire-raising traditionally took three forms:

wilful fire-raising, intentional fire-raising and reckless fire-raising, however, only two forms of fire-raising are now recognised by the courts, namely wilful fire-raising and reckless fire-raising. Either crime can be committed in respect of any type of property (*Byrne v. H.M. Advocate* (2000)).

WILFUL FIRE-RAISING

Wilful fire-raising requires that the accused intentionally set fire to property. The *mens rea*, therefore, is intention, and the *actus reus* is the setting fire to the property of another.

Before an accused can be convicted of wilful fire-raising in respect of any particular item of property, the Crown must establish beyond reasonable doubt that she intended to set fire to that item of property. This becomes more complex where an accused intends to set fire to an item within a property and unintentionally the fire spreads to the whole building. Such a scenario occurred in the case *Blane v. H.M. Advocate* (1991) where the accused set fire to a quilt in a room within a hostel. He gave evidence that he did this so that he could inhale the smoke and thereby commit suicide. He neither intended nor foresaw that the fire would spread as it did causing £15,000 worth of damage. On appeal, the court held that a conviction of wilful fire-raising required that the accused intended to set fire to the building or showed an utter disregard from which his intention could be inferred. This reference to utter disregard, *i.e.* a high degree of recklessness, as being equivalent to intention was subsequently overruled by *Byrne v. H.M. Advocate* (2000).

In *Byrne* a bench of five judges confirmed that the crime of wilful fire-raising requires a *mens rea* of intention and that no degree of recklessness will be treated as equivalent to intent. They also said that there was no place for the doctrine of transferred intention in the crime of fire-raising (see Chapter 2). The charges of wilful and reckless fire-raising are not inter-changeable, as they have different *mens rea*, so it is not possible to convict of one crime on a charge of the other. If the prosecution wish to have the option of either wilful or reckless fire-raising, it is necessary that both charges appear as alternatives on the indictment. Where there are alternative charges, a verdict of guilty can only be returned in respect of one of the charges.

RECKLESS FIRE-RAISING.

This crime involves recklessly setting fire to the property of another. The crime is not restricted to particular types of property. Reckless fire-raising could be charged, for example, if an accused set fire to his own property and this spread to an adjoining property.

READING

P. W. Ferguson, *Crimes Against the Person* (2nd ed., Butterworths, Edinburgh, 1998), Chap. 6.

C. Gane, C. Stoddart and J. Chalmers, *A Casebook on Scottish Criminal Law* (3rd ed., W. Green & Son, Edinburgh, 2001), Pt III.

G. H. Gordon, *Criminal Law* (3rd ed., M. Christie (ed.), W. Green & Son, Edinburgh, 2001), Vol. II.

T. Jones and M. Christie, *Criminal Law* (2nd ed., W. Green & Son, Edinburgh, 1996), Chaps 10 and 11.

R. McCall Smith and D. Sheldon, *Scots Criminal Law* (Butterworths, Edinburgh, 1997), Chaps 14–18.

---

5. CRIMES RELATING TO PUBLIC ORDER

Offences against public order include breach of the peace and mobbing. In this Chapter, offences against the state will also be considered.

BREACH OF THE PEACE

The definition of breach of the peace is so wide that it has been suggested that almost all of the criminal law of Scotland could fall within the definition (Jones and Christie, p. 316). Case law illustrates that acts which are in themselves both lawful, *e.g.* playing football in the street at night (*Cameron v. Normand* (1992)), and unlawful, *e.g.* assault, may be regarded as a breach of the peace. A breach of the peace may be committed in public or private. This crime has been used in Scots law to deal with modern nuisances that do not fall within the ambit of other crimes. Examples of this can be seen in relation to stalking and harassment which have been treated by the common law as amounting to a breach of the peace.

Actus Reus

The *actus reus* of this crime is conduct which "may reasonably be expected to cause any person to be alarmed, upset or annoyed or to provoke a disturbance of the peace" (*Wilson v. Brown* (1982), at p. 362). There is no requirement of evidence that the conduct caused alarm, upset or annoyance, merely that it had the potential to do so. In assessing whether conduct is capable of being classified as a breach of the peace an objective test is applied. In *Wyness v. Lockhart* (1992) the accused were convicted of breach of the peace by approaching two people in the street, offering to shake hands with them, patting them on the shoulder and asking them for money. Whilst none of the parties approached reported being alarmed, the convictions were confirmed on appeal because the conduct was such that might reasonably have resulted in alarm. In *Donaldson v. Vannet* (1998) the accused was convicted of breach of the peace as a result of stopping people in a busy street and asking for money. This conviction was quashed on appeal. Lord Johnston, delivering the opinion of the Court said (at p. 959):

> "[W]e think the *Wyness* case is distinguishable because there was physical contact with the potential victims. While we recognise in this case that the magistrate has found it proved that some of the persons approached were placed in a state of alarm, we do not consider that the findings are sufficient to show that the objective test has been met."

Mens Rea

Until recently the *mens rea* of breach of the peace has not been clearly defined. Some cases have gone so far as to almost suggest that it is a strict liability offence. There are few cases that have considered the *mens rea* of breach of the peace. In *Butcher v. Jessop* (1989) the appellant and three other accused (all footballers) were charged with conducting themselves in a disorderly manner and committing a breach of the peace during a football match. The appellant had pushed a player from the opposing side and the reaction of the supporters was such that it looked as if the field may be invaded. The court referred to Gordon's definition of the *mens rea* of this crime, namely, "it is not necessary to show that the accused intended to provoke a disturbance, it is enough that his conduct was such that the court regarded it as objectively calculated to do so" (*Criminal Law* (2nd ed., para. 41-09)). The court emphasised the importance of the accused's knowledge of the rivalry, animosity, excitement and tension between the fans of the two football teams.

In *Hughes v. Crowe* (1993) the court held that the *mens rea* of breach of the peace should be inferred from the nature and quality of the acts complained of. In this case the accused was charged with breach of the peace as a result of playing loud music and making noise in his flat between 7.15 a.m. and 8.15 a.m. on a Saturday morning. This had disturbed the occupants of the flat below. The court held (at p. 323) that:

> "[T]he time of day, the nature of the accommodation, the degree of noise and its duration all fall to be taken together in considering the essential question whether acts of the necessary nature and quality to establish a breach of the peace had been established. Treating this as a question of fact and degree primarily for the justice to decide, we cannot say that the decision which he reached was one which he was not entitled to reach on the evidence."

It is clear that the *mens rea* of breach of the peace is not intention or recklessness. Both cases suggest that the necessary *mens rea* of the crime is knowledge of the circumstances which may render the actions a breach of the peace. So in *Butcher* the accused's actions, the history of the relationship between the two football teams and the state of excitement of fans were the relevant circumstances. In *Hughes* the noise, the time of day and the location of his flat in close proximity to others were the relevant the circumstances.

MOBBING

Mobbing is committed by being part of a mob who act together with a common illegal purpose. The *mens rea* of mobbing is not dealt with explicitly in any cases, however, it clearly demands knowledge of the common purpose that is being pursued. The *actus reus* of mobbing has three elements: (1) there must be a number of people; (2) there must be a common illegal purpose; and (3) the conduct of the mob must cause public alarm and disturbance. The similarity between the crime of mobbing and the requirements of art and part liability is obvious. Where there is a common purpose to commit a particular crime then it would be competent to charge the accused art and part with that crime. For example, if in the course of mobbing a death results it is competent to charge the accused art and part with the crime of murder or, alternatively, mobbing. In this scenario the former is more likely as murder is a more serious crime attracting a mandatory life sentence.

Actus Reus

(1) There must be a number of people
There is not a specified minimum or maximum number of people required for mobbing, however, eight has been deemed to be an acceptable number (*Hancock v. H.M. Advocate* (1981)) and there has been a suggestion that five may be too few (*Sloan v. MacMillan* (1922)).

(2) There must be a common illegal purpose
A peaceful and legal common purpose would not fulfil the requirements of mobbing, instead the common purpose must be a violent or mischievous one (*Alexander McLean* (1886)). The common purpose does not require to be planned but can arise spontaneously, e.g. a peaceful and legal demonstration which becomes one involving a common illegal purpose (*George Smith* (1848)).

(3) Conduct of the mob must cause public alarm and disturbance
The conduct of the mob must cause significant public alarm and disturbance (Hume, i, 416).

OFFENCES AGAINST THE STATE

This group of offences does not have an official title. They include: treason, sedition, perjury, attempt to pervert the course of justice and giving false information to the authorities.

TREASON

This offence is only of importance in wartime or in time of rebellion. The offence involves a violation of allegiance to the government and the Crown. Offences against state security in peace time are generally not regarded as treason, but as specific statutory offences, *e.g.* breach of the Official Secrets Acts 1911–1989.

SEDITION

Like treason this crime is not significant in times of peace or stable government and is consequently, now rarely used. The crime, as described by Hume, suggests that any serious criticism of the Church, monarchy or government might amount to sedition if "suited and intended to disturb the tranquillity of the state,– for the purpose of producing trouble or commotion, ... resistance, or subversion, of the established government and laws." (Hume, i, 553)

PERJURY

This common law crime involves the judicial affirmation of falsehood upon oath (Hume, i, 369). So, if a witness lies under oath she can be convicted of perjury if the evidence she gave was pertinent to the point at issue. The *actus reus* of the offence is the giving of the evidence and the *mens rea* is the knowledge that it is not true.

ATTEMPT TO PERVERT OR DEFEAT OR HINDER THE COURSE OF JUSTICE

Note these are completed crimes and not criminal attempts. The word attempt is used in a descriptive rather than a legal sense. The *mens rea* is intention to pervert the course of justice.

GIVING FALSE INFORMATION TO THE AUTHORITIES

This could be classified as an attempt to pervert the course of justice but, as it normally involves information at the beginning of an investigation rather than contributing to an investigation which is ongoing, the tendency is to charge it as a crime in its own right. The crime takes two forms:

(1) Making a false accusation of crime against a particular named individual.

(2) Giving of false information to the police or procurator fiscal which results in an investigation. This is sometimes referred to as wasting police time. The *mens rea* is intention and knowledge that the information is false.

READING

C. Gane, C. Stoddart and J. Chalmers, *A Casebook on Scottish Criminal Law* (3rd ed., W. Green & Son, Edinburgh, 2001), Pt IV.

G. H. Gordon, *Criminal Law* (3rd ed., M. Christie (ed.), W. Green & Son, Edinburgh, 2001), Vol. II.

T. Jones and M. Christie, *Criminal Law* (2nd ed., W. Green & Son, Edinburgh, 1996), Chap. 12.

---

6. DEFENCES

Criminal defences are an essential element of any legal system. Defences can result in an accused being acquitted or, alternatively, their criminal responsibility being mitigated.

Criminal defences operate in one of three ways. First, they may justify the accused's behaviour and result in acquittal even although the prosecution have proved each element in the definition of the crime—these are often referred to as justifying defences and would include self-defence, coercion and necessity.

Secondly, there are defences that operate to excuse the actions of the accused. In such cases, the elements of the definition of the crime have been proved by the prosecution but because of some excusing condition the accused cannot be held fully responsible for her actions. Excuses are recognised where the accused has committed an unjustifiable act but cannot be regarded as morally blameworthy, *e.g.* an accused who pleads insanity to a charge of murder does not claim that she was justified in killing but rather that she is not morally blameworthy due to her mental condition. These defences are often referred to as excuses and include insanity and provocation. Note that some excusing defences will result in acquittal, *e.g.* insanity, or to mitigate the crime, *e.g.* from murder to culpable homicide in the case of provocation.

Thirdly, they may raise a reasonable doubt concerning a material element of the prosecution's case, *e.g.* the defence of alibi establishes that the accused did not in fact perpetuate the *actus reus* of the crime.

Note that as well as these formal methods of mitigating responsibility, a plea in mitigation may be presented to the court on behalf of the accused. This will take place after the accused has either pled or been found guilty and is done with the purpose of lessening the punishment to be given. An accused is also entitled to introduce evidence of mitigating circumstances in the course of his trial.

SPECIAL DEFENCES

Criminal defences are not only distinguished by the ways in which they operate but also in the procedure attached to them in court. The term "special defence" is a procedural term and refers to the defences which an accused is not allowed to state unless written notice has been lodged at least 10 clear days before the trial, except where the accused is able to satisfy the court that there was good reason for not having done so. In addition to sharing this procedural rule special defences are those which Lord Walker in *Adam v. Macneill* (1972) said "put in issue a fact (1) which is not referred to in the libel, and (2) which, if established, necessarily results in acquittal of the accused." Note that acquittal can also result from the defence of necessity but this defence does not require to be notified to the court 10 clear days before the trial. There is no definite list of special defences, however, it includes the following:

(1) Alibi
(2) Incrimination
(3) Insanity
(4) Self-defence
(5) Automatism
(6) Coercion

(1) Alibi
This defence is simply that at the time of the offence the accused was not at the place libelled. If such a defence is lodged it must be relevant and, therefore, specify where the accused was, and at what time.

(2) Incrimination
The defence of incrimination involves a claim that the crime was not committed by the accused but by another person, who is named if they are known. It is not a special defence where the accused attempts to incriminate his co-accused. In this instance, however, notice of intention to lead evidence to support such a claim must be lodged with the court.

(3) Insanity
Insanity is used in pleadings in criminal law in two ways. First, it is used as a plea in bar of trial and, secondly, as a special defence. It is important, however, to note at the outset that insanity is purely a legal concept. Insanity is not a medical term and is not a form of mental disorder. In *Brennan v. H.M. Advocate* (1977), Lord Emslie said (at p. 42) that the concept of insanity was not to be resolved upon medical opinion. It is, on the contrary, a question which has to be

resolved by the law itself as a matter of legal policy in order to set, in the public interest, acceptable limits upon the circumstances in which any person may be able to relieve himself of criminal responsibility.

Plea in Bar of Trial

This is not a special defence but will normally be a preliminary plea, *i.e.* a plea that is heard before the trial commences, to prevent the trial proceeding because the accused is unfit to plead. Notice of such a preliminary plea requires to be given to the court at least 10 days in advance of the trial starting. The test used to determine if an accused is unfit to plead is a culmination of three individual judicial decisions:

(a) whether the accused is able to instruct legal advisers and tell them fully about his actions (*Brown* (1907));
(b) whether the accused can tell his counsel what his defence is and whether the accused understands the proceedings (*H.M. Advocate v. Wilson* 1942)); and
(c) whether there is such a degree of unfairness to the appellant/accused that she is not a fit object for trial. (*Russell v. H.M. Advocate* (1946)).

The provisions governing the process to deal with a plea in bar of trial and the disposals available to the court are contained in sections 52–63 of the Criminal Procedure (Scotland) Act 1995 (hereinafter referred to as the "1995 Act") which came into force on April 1, 1996. Unfitness to plead is usually raised by the defence or the prosecution by way of a preliminary plea. The onus of proof will lie with whichever party alleges the accused is unfit to plead. If, during the course of a trial, it appears that a person is unfit to plead then the question may raised by the defence, prosecution or the judge/sheriff. Before an accused can be found unfit to plead there must be corroborating evidence from at least two psychiatrists. The preliminary diet to determine fitness to plead is held outwith the presence of a jury and the decision is made by the presiding sheriff or judge.

If an accused is found unfit to plead instead of a trial there is an "examination of the facts". At the examination of the facts the court shall, on the basis of evidence given, determine whether it is satisfied beyond reasonable doubt that (i) the accused committed the offence charged, and (ii) that on the balance of probabilities that there are no grounds for acquitting her. The court may also (iii) acquit the person on the grounds that they were insane when they committed the offence. If any of these conclusions are reached, then section 57 provides that the following methods of disposal are open to the court:

(a) a hospital order—in a hospital the court specifies;
(b) a hospital order without limit of time. This is compulsory where there is a charge of murder;
(c) make a guardianship order placing the person under the guardianship of the local authority;

(d) make a supervision and treatment order; or
(e) make no order.

Alternatively, if the court determine that the accused did not commit the offence charged then the accused will be acquitted and will be free to go.

Prior to the 1995 Act the plea in bar of trial was governed by the provisions of the Criminal Procedure (Scotland) Act 1975. Under the old provisions where a plea in bar of trial was successful, the accused was detained in the state hospital or such other hospital as the court specified. The effect of this provision was that an accused could spend an unlimited amount of time in hospital without it ever having been established that they committed the crime with which they had been charged.

Insanity as a Special Defence

The insanity defence differs from the plea in bar of trial. As it is a special defence, the accused must give the court notice that the defence will be pled at least 10 days in advance of the trial starting. The defence is pled in the course of a normal trial and the only variation on normal procedure is that the onus of proof switches to the defence, but only for the purpose of proving the insanity defence.

What is Required for the Insanity Defence? The Scottish definition of insanity is derived from Hume (i, 37) who stated that:

> "To serve the purpose of a defence in law, the disorder must ... amount to an absolute alienation of reason ... such a disease as deprives the patient of the knowledge of the true aspect and position of things about him—hinders him from distinguishing friend or foe—and gives him up to the impulse of his own distempered fancy."

This definition has formed the basis of subsequent judge's directions to juries. In *H.M. Advocate v. Kidd* (1960) the accused was charged with the murder of his wife and daughter by administering chloroform to them and asphyxiating them. Lord Strachan directed the jury that (at p. 70):

> "The question really is this, whether at the time of the offences charged the accused was of unsound mind ... The question is one primarily of fact ... First, in order to excuse a person from responsibility for his acts on the ground of insanity, there must have been an alienation of reason in relation to the act committed. There must have been some mental defect ... by which his reason was overpowered and he was thereby rendered incapable of exerting his reason to control his conduct and reactions."

Difference Between the Insanity Defence and the Plea in Bar of Trial. In *Kidd*, Lord Strachan distinguished the plea in bar of trial and the insanity defence. He directed the jury (at p. 62):

"You are ... concerned with his mental condition at the time of the alleged offences. It is not suggested that the accused is insane now, and you must proceed upon the footing that he is now sane. If he were insane now he could not have given instructions for his defence, and the case would not have proceeded before you in the form in which it has taken."

This direction distinguishes the plea in bar of trial which, if successful, would have prevented the trial proceeding and the insanity defence which necessitates that the accused was insane at the time of the alleged offences but that he is sane at the time of the trial.

Burden of Proof. Where the insanity defence is pled the burden of proof lies on the accused in respect of proving insanity. The accused is presumed to be sane unless he proves that he was insane. The standard of proof required is, however, lower than for the prosecution. Whereas the latter must prove beyond reasonable doubt that the accused committed the crime charged, the defence of insanity requires to be proven on the balance of probability.

Role of Medical Evidence in Proving Insanity. Insanity is a matter for the jury to determine. The definition of insanity and the role of medical evidence was confirmed in *Kidd*. Lord Strachan directed the jury in *Kidd* (at p. 70) that:

"[T]he question [of insanity] is to be decided by you in the light of the evidence, in the exercise of your commonsense and knowledge of mankind, and it is to be judged on the ordinary rules on which men act in daily life. Thirdly, the question is to be decided in the light of the whole circumstances disclosed in the evidence ... the medical evidence by itself is not conclusive."

Intoxication and Insanity. The question of whether "a complete alienation of reason" could be induced by drugs and alcohol was raised in *Brennan v. H.M. Advocate* (1977). In *Brennan*, the appellant was convicted of murdering his father by stabbing him. On the day of the killing the appellant had consumed between 20 and 25 pints of beer, a glass of sherry and about half an hour before the killing, a microdot of LSD. The special defence of insanity had been lodged and it was contended that the effect of the self-induced intoxication might be to reduce the crime from murder to culpable homicide. The trial judge directed the jury that the evidence of the accused's state of intoxication did not entitle them to return a verdict of culpable homicide. At the trial, the judge withdrew the defence of insanity from the jury. The accused was convicted and appealed on the ground that self-induced intoxication of a sufficient degree can amount to insanity. Further, even if there is insufficient evidence of insanity, the appellant argued that it was a question for the jury whether the accused was so intoxicated as to be legally insane at the time of the alleged crime, or whether his actions amounted to culpable homicide rather than murder.

This appeal was heard by a bench of seven judges. Rejecting the first ground of appeal they said (at p. 153):

> "In short, insanity in our law requires proof of total alienation of reason in relation to the act charged as the result of mental illness, mental disease or defect or unsoundness of mind and does not comprehend the malfunctioning of transitory effect, as the result of deliberate and self-induced intoxication."

The second ground of appeal was that the appellant was intoxicated to such a degree that he was deprived of all capacity to form the "specific intent" which is of the essence of the crime of murder. The Court reiterated that self-induced intoxication, whatever the degree, is not insanity and cannot support a defence of diminished responsibility, and that in these areas the law of Scotland is consistent with Hume and Alison (at p. 155) that "self-induced intoxication is no defence to any criminal charge, at least for an offence in itself perilous or hurtful."

(4) Self-defence

Self-defence is available where an accused uses physical force to protect herself, or a third party, from an attack by the complainer. Self-defence can be pled in relation to both a charge of assault and homicide. The rules are the same in both contexts, except that where self-defence is used in response to an assault, there does not need to be imminent danger of death but merely imminent danger of serious injury. As self-defence can serve to justify a fatal attack on another person it is not surprising that the rules of this defence are rather restricted. In the case of homicide the essential elements are:

- the accused was in imminent danger to life;
- the accused was unable to escape; and
- the degree of violence used in self-defence was not excessive.

The requirements are, therefore, that any threat to life must be imminent and, therefore, threats of future injury will not be enough. Second, if there is a means of escape then the individual is under a duty to use it. Third, the force used must be both necessary in the circumstances and also proportional to the threat. In *Fenning v. H.M. Advocate* (1985) Lord Cameron said (at p. 225):

> "While the law permits the use of force in repelling force when escape from the attacker is not reasonably possible, the protection which the law affords to the victim of an attack is not a licence to use force grossly in excess of that necessary to defend himself ... That is the foundation on which the plea itself is based. What is that excess in a particular case is a matter for the jury to decide on the evidence before them and under proper and sufficient direction in law."

The issue of proportionate retaliation is complex, however, directions to juries have shed some light on the requirements. In *H.M. Advocate v. Doherty* (1954) the accused was charged with the culpable homicide of a man called Cairns, by stabbing him in the eye with a bayonet. A means of escape existed at the time so that retreat would have been possible. A special defence of self-defence was lodged by the accused. Doherty claimed that he killed Cairns while defending himself from a hammer attack. On the question of proportionate retaliation, Lord Keith directed the jury (at pp. 4–5):

> "You do not need an exact proportion of injury and retaliation; it is not a matter that you weigh in too fine scales ... Some allowance must be made for the excitement or the state of fear or the heat of blood at the moment of the man who is attacked, but there are limits or tests that are perfectly well recognised that will help you to understand this doctrine by way of illustration. For instance, if a man was struck a blow by another man with the fist, that could not justify retaliation by the use of a knife, because there is no real proportion at all between a blow with a fist and retaliation by a knife, and therefore, you have got to consider this question of proportion between the attack made and the retaliation offered."

Self-defence and Rape

The exception to the requirement that an accused must be in imminent danger of life before self-defence can be pled, is where a woman is resisting an attack of rape. As noted in Chapter 3, rape, in Scots law, is a crime that can only be committed against a woman. As a consequence, retaliation to an attack of rape is only available to a woman, or people assisting her to resist an attack, and has not been extended to men defending themselves from an attack of sodomy.

In *McCluskey v. H.M. Advocate* (1959) the accused was charged with the murder of a man called Ormiston. He pled self-defence on the grounds that he killed the deceased while resisting an attempt by the latter to commit sodomy upon him. Lord Strachan gave the following direction (at p. 40) at the trial to the jury on the question of self-defence :

> "Speaking generally, homicide will not be justified by self-defence unless it is committed of necessity in the just apprehension on the part of the killer that he cannot otherwise save his own life only if the homicidal acts are done to save the man's own life ... It does not bring the accused within the plea of self-defence if he kills to avoid some great indignity, some attack upon his virtue, or even some bodily harm."

The jury returned a verdict of guilty of culpable homicide, presumably on the grounds of provocation. The accused appealed on the grounds that the judge had misdirected the jury. At appeal Lord Clyde confirmed (at p. 42) the view of Alison (i, 132) that:

> "A private individual will be justified in killing in defence of his life against imminent danger, of the lives of others connected with him from similar peril, or a woman or her friends in resisting an attempt at rape. It seems to me impossible to assimilate the present case to a woman threatened with rape. For rape involves complete absence of consent on the part of the woman. This is not the situation in sodomy."

McCluskey confirms that self-defence can be used to protect third parties from imminent danger of serious injury (in response to a charge of assault) or death (in response to a charge of homicide) or by third parties or the woman herself in resisting an attack of rape. The refusal by the court to recognise the defence in respect of retaliation to sodomy was confirmed in *Elliott v. H.M. Advocate* (1987).

Mistaken Belief and Self-defence

The question of mistaken belief and self-defence will arise where an accused mistakenly believes that they are in imminent danger of life. In *Owens v. H.M. Advocate* (1946) the accused believed that the deceased was attacking him with a knife and killed him. He was convicted of murder, but on appeal the conviction was quashed on the grounds that the appellant's belief that he was in imminent danger was held on reasonable grounds. Lord Justice-General Normand stated (at p. 125):

> "[S]elf defence is made out when it is established to the satisfaction of the jury that the [accused] believed that he was in imminent danger and that he held that belief on reasonable grounds. Grounds for such belief may exist though they are founded on a genuine mistake of fact."

A mistaken belief in respect of a fatal attack must be both honest and reasonable to be successful. This is tested objectively, and is distinct from the approach adopted in rape cases (see Chapter 3 and *Meek v. H.M. Advocate* (1982)).

Self–defence and Property

There is not a great deal of Scottish authority on whether self-defence can be used in defence of property, however, in the case McCluskey discussed above, Lord Clyde implicitly excludes killing in the defence of property in his description of when the defence could be pled. It is unlikely, however, that a person who struggles with a thief who is trying to steal a bag will be charged with assault, however, if a housebreaker was severely assaulted with, *e.g.* a weapon, the situation would differ and self-defence would not be available.

Is Self-defence Available where the Accused has Started a Fight?

Self-defence may be open to a person who has started an altercation. The normal rules of self-defence, outlined above, would apply in these circumstances. In *Boyle v. H.M. Advocate* (1993) the court held that the trial judge had misdirected the jury when he said the appellant could not plead self-defence if he willingly joined the fight he was involved in and that the availability of self-defence would depend on the circumstances. This was followed in *Burns v. H.M. Advocate* (1995) which reiterated that the issue is whether the victim's response to the accused's initial violence is of the quality to place the accused in immediate danger of life and that he then responds proportionately when there is no means of escape.

(5) Automatism

A person who acts in a state of unconsciousness or grossly impaired consciousness, may be said to act as an automaton and a defence of automatism may be available. Automatism cases commonly involve somnambulism, diabetes, epileptic seizure and the effect of ingesting certain types of drugs. The Criminal Procedure (Scotland) Act 1995, s.78(2), defined automatism as a special defence. The question of automatism is rather complex. The first issue that should be noted is that automatism is distinct from insanity. The latter requires mental illness or a mental disorder that results in a total alienation of reason, automatism, on the other hand, is where the accused's mental state is caused by external factors. Automatism was not recognised as a defence prior to 1991, and to operate as a defence very strict conditions must be complied with. The defence has been interpreted to negate the *mens rea* of the accused rather than the *actus reus*. This has implications for those strict liability offences where *mens rea* does not require to be proven.

Requirements of Automatism Prior to Ross
Until *Ross v. H.M. Advocate* (1991) the law in Scotland, in respect of automatic acts, was governed by *H.M. Advocate v. Cunningham* (1963). In *Cunningham*, the accused was charged with taking a motorvan, causing death by dangerous driving and being unfit to drive through drink or drugs. He lodged a special defence, which stated that (at p. 80):

"[T]hroughout the period during which the crimes libelled are said to have been committed he was not responsible for his actings on account of the incidence of temporary dissociation due to an epileptic fugue or other pathological condition."

Lord Justice-General Clyde (at p. 83) rejected that this was a competent special defence at all and stated that these factors only had a bearing upon mitigation of sentence and not upon guilt. He said that to be accepted as a special defence this would require an averment of insanity at the time the offence was committed and, if successful, it would result in the accused's detention in the State Hospital. He stated (at p. 84) that:

"Any mental or pathological condition short of insanity—any question of diminished responsibility owing to any cause, which does not involve insanity—is relevant only to the question of mitigating circumstances and sentence."

In *Cunningham*, the Crown argued that *H.M. Advocate v. Ritchie* (1926), where the defence of temporary mental dissociation due to toxic exhaust fumes was accepted as a special defence, could be distinguished due to the exhaust fumes being an external factor. Lord Clyde concluded, however, that *Ritchie* had been wrongly decided.

The effect of the decision in *Cunningham* was that, unless temporary mental dissociation met the legal requirements of the defence of insanity (with the consequences, prior to the 1995 Act, of detention in hospital), it could not mitigate responsibility but only the punishment of the accused. Therefore, those who committed crimes while in a state of involuntary intoxication, concussion, epilepsy or diabetes had no defence available to them. This was even though they clearly lacked the necessary *mens rea* to commit crimes and their actions were not in any sense voluntary. *Ross v. H.M. Advocate* (1991) has partially overruled *Cunningham* but there remain circumstances, *e.g.* where the accused's actions are the result of an internal condition, such as epilepsy or diabetes, when *Cunningham* remains the authoritative case.

Ross v. H.M. Advocate

In *Ross*, the accused was charged with a number of assaults. His defence was that his drink had been "spiked" with hallucinogenic and tranquillising drugs, that he did not know his drink had been spiked and that it was this, which had caused his violent conduct. The defence argued that the effect of the drugs was to deprive the accused of his self-control to such an extent that he was incapable of forming *mens rea* and that it should be left to the jury to consider whether or not they should acquit him on this ground. The trial judge directed the jury, in accordance with *Cunningham*, that the evidence of the accused's mental state at the time could not result in acquittal. Ross was convicted and appealed on the grounds that the jury had been misdirected to convict the accused; that the judge was wrong in holding that he was bound by *Cunningham*, and if *Cunningham* was held to apply it should be reconsidered in order that a defence of non-culpable automatism be admissible.

The court noted that senior counsel for the appellant did not seek to challenge the soundness of *Cunningham* on its own facts. Lord Justice-General Hope noted (at p. 213) that "in principle it would seem that in all cases where a person lacks the evil intention which is essential to the guilt of crime he must be acquitted." Two exceptions to this principle were identified. Senior counsel and the judges recognised that where the mental condition which is said to affect *mens rea* is a pathological condition which might recur, it must for reasons of public policy, be the subject of a special defence of insanity. Lord Hope also stated at (p. 214) that where the absence of *mens rea* is self-induced the accused must, for public policy reasons, be assumed to have intended the natural consequences of his act.

However, the court in *Ross* emphasised that there was no challenge to *Cunningham* on its facts, as *Ross* was concerned with a mental condition of a temporary nature which was the result of an external factor which was not self-induced, and it did not involve a disorder of the mind that was liable to recur. In *Ross*, Lord Hope (at p. 218) provided the following requirements before automatism would result in acquittal, and stated that these should provide adequate safeguards against abuse. The requirements are:

(a)   the external factor must not be self-induced;

(b)   it must be one which the accused was not bound to foresee; and

(c) it must have resulted in a total alienation of reason amounting to a complete absence of self-control.

The principle of *Ross* was followed in the case *Sorley v. H.M. Advocate* (1992). *Sorley* establishes that the evidential burden on the accused who pleads this defence is a heavy one. There must be expert evidence of a total alienation of reason leading to a complete loss of self-control and the evidence must show that the accused did not know the nature of his actions.

Effect of Ross
The effect of the decision in *Ross* was to partially over-turn the decision in *Cunningham*. As a result, any internal condition, *e.g.* epilepsy, diabetes or somnambulism (*Simon Fraser*), which is the cause of an automatic state will only be relevant in determining sentence and not responsibility, unless the accused also happens to be insane when they commit the offence. As noted above, where an automatic state is the result of self-induced intoxication by alcohol or drugs, even where intoxication has induced a state such as parasomnia, the defence of automatism is not available to an accused (*Finnegan v. Heywood* (2000); *Ebsworth v. H.M. Advocate* (1992)).

The matter is more complicated where a diabetic person offends as a result of insulin induced hypoglycaemia. *Ross* suggested that hypoglycaemia is not a proper basis for a defence of automatism but this was not followed in *MacLeod v. Mathieson* (1993), nor in *H.M. Advocate v. Watret* (unreported, Kilmarnock High Court, October 1999). In *Watret*, Lord Nimmo Smith directed the jury that, as far as he was aware, this was the first time the High Court had considered the defence of automatism arising from alleged hypoglycaemia. The accused was indicted on four charges of breach of the peace and one charge of aggravated assault and attempted murder. Three of the breach of the peace charges related to the period when the accused was on bail, pending his trial for the aggravated assault and attempted murder charge. In the course of an argument, Watret had attacked his wife with a Stanley knife which resulted in her being permanently scarred. The accused's defence was that he was in a hypoglycaemic state at the time of the attack. The advocate-depute invited the judge to direct the jury that the special defence of automatism was not open for their consideration. The judge repelled this submission and directed the jury on the three requirements of automatism. The jury were asked to decide whether hypoglycaemia is ever capable of amounting to automatism. In particular they were asked to consider:

(1) Whether insulin could properly be described as an external factor and while it may be self-administered, as it is not in general taken for the purposes of causing hypoglycaemia, is it self-induced? (This question was to address whether the taking of the insulin was an external factor that was not self-induced.)

(2) Was the accused bound to foresee the possibility of insulin as an external factor, causing such a degree of hypoglycaemia as to result in a total alienation of reason, amounting to a total loss of control of his actions? To answer this question the jury were asked to consider his level of knowledge and what advice had been given to the accused about matters such as the interval of time between taking insulin and taking food, the effects of alcohol on blood sugar levels, and so on. (This question was to ascertain whether the effects of the insulin were reasonably foreseeable.)

(3) In light of the expert evidence whether a hypoglycaemic attack amounts to a total alienation of reason. (This question is to establish if the effect of the insulin was to cause a total alienation of reason.)

The accused was found guilty of two of the breach of the peace charges and the aggravated assault charge under deletion of "to the danger of life and you did attempt to murder her" with the added rider "whilst in a hypoglycaemic state". The jury clearly did not accept that the accused fulfilled the requirements of the automatism defence or they would have acquitted him, however, Lord Nimmo Smith did say that the rider was taken into account in passing a sentence of imprisonment of three years.

(6) Coercion

Coercion arises where one person has forced another to commit a crime. It may operate either as a defence or in mitigation. It is now classified as a special defence by the Criminal Procedure (Scotland) Act 1995, s.78(2).

The rules of the defence are outlined by Hume (i, 51) as:

(a) there must be an immediate danger of death or great bodily harm;
(b) an inability to resist the violence;
(c) a backward and inferior part in the perpetration; and
(d) a disclosure of the fact, as well as restitution of the spoil, on the first safe and convenient occasion.

In *Thomson v. H.M. Advocate* (1983) the appellant was convicted art and part with another man of assault and armed robbery. Thomson claimed on the outward journey that he didn't know he was driving his co-accused to commit a robbery. When he found out and tried to leave, a gun was produced which went off when he tried to get out of the van and he was shot on the hand. His defence was that he had been coerced into taking part in the assault and robbery. The question of coercion was left to the jury, and Lord Hunter directed them on Hume's requirements for coercion and emphasised that there must be an immediate danger of death or great bodily harm. The jury convicted both accused. Thomson appealed on the ground that the judge had misdirected the jury as to the requirements of the defence of coercion. Refusing the appeal, Lord Justice-Clerk Wheatley stated that (at pp. 77–78):

"[T]he four 'qualifications' to which [Hume] refers are tests of the validity of such a defence. The first two are conditions to be satisfied before the defence gets off the ground. It is only if it does get off the ground that the other two tests come into play as a measure of the accused's credibility and reliability on the issue of the defence."

Coercion and Murder
It is unclear whether coercion would ever be a valid defence to murder. In *Thomson*, Lord Justice-Clerk Wheatley stated (at p. 78);
"[A] defence of coercion is recognised in the law of Scotland. Doubts have been expressed on whether it extends to murder cases, but that does not arise here and we express no opinion on that point. Hume restricts it to 'atrocious crimes', and whether a particular crime falls into that category will depend not only on the nature of the crime but on its attendant circumstances."
In *Collins v. H.M. Advocate* (1991) Lord Allanbridge directed the jury that (at p. 902) "as a matter of law coercion is not a defence in Scotland to the crime of murder".

OTHER DEFENCES

In addition to the "special defences" outlined above, there are other defences which do not require notice to be given to the court. The defences is this group serve to mitigate responsibility of the accused but do not result in acquittal.

Diminished Responsibility
Diminished responsibility, unlike insanity, does not result in the acquittal of the accused but only mitigates the accused's responsibility. The defence has been viewed as only being available in respect of a charge of murder and, where it is successfully pled, results in a conviction of culpable homicide. When diminished responsibility is pled, the onus of proof is on the defence for the purpose of proving diminished responsibility. Diminished responsibility requires to be proven on the balance of probability.

The doctrine of diminished responsibility, rather than the term, first appeared in *H.M. Advocate v. Dingwall* (1867) where the accused had stabbed his wife to death when she had apparently hidden drink from him. He was charged with murder and pled insanity. On the basis that he had suffered sun-stroke and later convulsions when serving with the British Army in India, medical witnesses said that he was "weak minded, wayward and eccentric" but the deciding factor was that he was an alcoholic and regularly suffered from delirium. The judge directed the jury that the weakness of mind might be due to alcohol and, although there were not grounds for an acquittal on the basis of insanity, they could consider a verdict of culpable homicide. The jury returned a verdict of culpable homicide and *Dingwall* was sentenced to 10 years' imprisonment.

The modern doctrine of diminished responsibility was regarded as being found in *H.M. Advocate v. Savage* (1923). In *Savage*, the accused was charged with murder of a woman by cutting her throat with a razor or other sharp instrument. Evidence was led on behalf of the accused that he had suffered an injury to his head in the past and that he was in the habit of indulging to excess in alcohol, was constantly under its influence and at times he drank methylated spirits which had the effect of making him violent and irresponsible. Witnesses spoke to him being under the influence of methylated spirits or alcohol on the night of the murder. Lord Justice-Clerk Alness directed the jury (at p. 51) that in order to reduce the quality of the accused's act from murder to culpable homicide:

"[There] must be aberration or weakness of mind; that there must be some form of mental unsoundness; that there must be a state of mind which is bordering on, though not amounting to, insanity; that there must be a mind so affected that responsibility is diminished from full responsibility to partial responsibility—in other words, the prisoner in question must be only partially accountable for his actions. And I think that one can see running through the cases that there is implied ... that there must be some form of mental disease."

In the subsequent case *Connelly v. H.M. Advocate* (1990) the Appeal Court held that the requirements of diminished responsibility were correctly stated in *Savage* and that the passage, quoted above, must be read as a whole, and that there must be evidence of some form of mental disease.

Until *Galbraith v. H.M. Advocate* (2001) the direction to the jury in *Savage* was deemed to be authoritative. In *Galbraith*, the accused was charged with the murder of her husband. She admitted killing her husband but contended that she had been suffering from diminished responsibility at the time, due to years of abuse by her husband, and that she should be convicted of culpable homicide. At trial she was convicted of murder. She appealed against conviction on three grounds, including that the trial judge had misdirected the jury when he told them that they would have to find that the appellant was suffering from "some form of mental disease" before they could find the defence of diminished responsibility established. A bench of five judges ruled that in the case of *Connelly* the Court were wrong to insist that the passage from *Savage* had to be read as a whole and that all of the criteria had to be met. The Court overruled the decision in *Connelly* and held that the trial judge's direction in *Galbraith* was unsound. The Court held that while the plea of diminished responsibility will only be available where the accused's abnormality of mind had substantial effects in relation to his act, there is no requirement that his state of mind should have bordered on insanity. In terms of an appropriate direction to a jury on the question of diminished responsibility, it is stated that this should no longer simply recite the *Savage* formula, quoted above, but should be tailored as far as possible to the facts of the particular case (at p. 552):

"[I]n essence, the jury should be told that they must be satisfied that, by reason of the abnormality of mind in question, the ability of the accused, as compared with a normal person, to determine or control his actings was substantially impaired".

Galbraith's murder conviction was quashed and a re-trial was ordered.

Provocation

"The defence of provocation is of this sort:– Being agitated and excited, and alarmed by violence, I lost control over myself, and took life when my presence of mind had left me, and without thought of what I was doing" (Macdonald, *A Practical Treatise on the Criminal Law of Scotland* (5th ed.), p. 94).

The defence of provocation does not result in acquittal but operates as an excuse and will reduce a charge of murder to culpable homicide. In *Drury v. H.M. Advocate* (2001) Lord Justice-General Rodger stated (at p. 593) that:

"[T]he person who kills under provocation is to be convicted of culpable homicide rather than murder because, even if he intentionally kills his victim, he does not have that wicked intention which is required for murder."

A sucessful plea of provocation will reduce a charge of attempted murder to assault and mitigate the punishment in a charge of assault. The provocation must result in a total loss of self-control and any retaliation must be immediate and proportionate. Where the accused is charged with murder, any provocation must be by real injury. Verbal provocation is recognised in relation to assault but only where the provocation is immediate inflammatory abuse which leads to a loss of self-control (*Thomson v. H.M. Advocate* (1985)). There are similarities between the requirements of self-defence and provocation. The two defences are often pled together, however, they are separate and only self-defence is a special defence. The effect of a plea of provocation on a charge of murder is discussed in Chapter 3.

The institutional writers all recognise one exception to the rule that only provocation of the nature of serious assault is relevant to reduce a charge of murder to one of culpable homicide. This exception is where a person kills his/her spouse or paramour under the provocation of finding them in adultery(Hume, i, 245).

Rules of Provocation

Provocation must be by Real Injury and therefore Verbal Provocation is not enough. The general rule is that verbal provocation is not enough to reduce a charge of murder to culpable homicide (*Cosgrove v. H.M. Advocate* (1991)). Despite this, the courts have sometimes allowed juries to consider verbal provocation. In *Berry v.*

H.M. Advocate (1976) the accused was charged with the murder of a woman. He gave evidence that the deceased had taunted him when he had tried unsuccessfully to have intercourse with her, and that he had retaliated by striking her on the head with a brick. The trial judge allowed the question of provocation to be decided by the jury and directed them to consider whether these taunts were sufficient provocation for what the accused had done. The accused was convicted and appealed. Rejecting the appeal, the court expressed "grave doubts" regarding this issue having been left to the jury.

Provocation must Result in a Complete Loss of Self-control. Evidence of a loss of self-control is essential in any plea of provocation (*Low v. H.M. Advocate* (1994)). In addition to evidence, however, it also must be established that such a loss of self-control was reasonable. This has traditionally been tested objectively by reference to the reasonable person test. In *Drury v. H.M. Advocate* (2001) Lord Justice-General Rodger stated (at p. 599):

"[I]f there is evidence of a relationship entitling the accused to expect sexual fidelity on the part of the deceased, the jury should be directed to consider two matters. First, they should consider whether, at the time when he killed the deceased, the accused had in fact lost his self-control as a result of the preceding provocation. If they conclude that he had not lost his self-control, then the plea of provocation must fail and the jury will have to consider, on the basis of all the rest of the evidence, whether the appropriate verdict is one of murder or culpable homicide. If, on the other hand, the jury come to the conclusion that he had indeed lost his self-control due to the provocation, then they should ask themselves whether an ordinary man, having been thus provoked, would have been liable to react as he did."

This objective test, based on the ordinary person, does not take into account the characteristics of the accused. In other jurisdictions the accused's characteristics are considered in respect of both the effect of and the reaction to provocation, *e.g. R. v. Camplin* (1978). In those cases where the accused's characteristics are taken into account a subjective test is employed.

Retaliation must be Immediate. As any retaliation must be immediate, any time lapse between the provocation and retaliation may suggest that the accused has regained control and is merely taking revenge. Cumulative provocation is not recognised and, therefore, there must be a final provoking act before events that have occurred in the past are deemed relevant. This is particularly problematic where there has been a relationship between the accused and the deceased involving abuse and violence. In this situation, the perpetrator of fatal violence may anticipate, through past experience, that the deceased will become violent and act almost pre-emptively.

The difficulty in such a scenario is that the past violence is not recognised as being a reasonable basis to anticipate future events, nor is it deemed to amount to cumulative provocation in the absence of a final act of violence. Such a scenario is found in cases where women kill abusive men. In *H.M. Advocate v. June Greig* (1979) there was a history of abuse by the deceased towards his wife. On the night he was killed, the husband had been verbally, although not physically, abusive, and the accused's evidence was that she anticipated he would become violent. The judge in this case withdrew self-defence from the jury and directed the jury that there were no grounds for provocation. The jury, clearly ignoring his direction, returned a verdict of culpable homicide.

Retaliation must not have been Grossly Excessive. The retaliation to physical or verbal provocation must be proportionate. In determining the requirements of proportionate retaliation, the courts, in the past, adopted a similar approach to that used in respect of self-defence. For both self-defence and provocation, therefore, if an accused had acted with "cruel excess" neither provocation nor self-defence was available to them. In *Lennon v. H.M. Advocate* (1991) (at p. 614F), Lord Justice-General Hope refers to "cruel excess, or a gross disproportion between the provocation offered and the retaliation" excluding provocation. Subsequent case law suggests that the preferred test for provocation is "gross disproportion" (*Robertson v. H.M. Advocate* (1994)). This matter is more complex where the provocation is the discovery of adultery, which is considered below.

Adultery Exception
There is one exception to the rule that only provocation by physical violence is relevant to a charge of murder. This exception is the adultery exception. Hume referred to provocation applying where the accused discovered his wife committing adultery with a man. Later cases also recognised an admission of adultery (*H.M. Advocate v. Hill* (1941)), a suspicion that adultery had or was about to take place (*H.M. Advocate v. Gilmour* (1937)), where the parties were not married but it was deemed that sexual fidelity was owed (*McDermott v. H.M. Advocate* (1974)), where the couple were of the same sex (*H.M. Advocate v. Kean* (1996)) and where there had been confessions of past adultery (*Rutherford v. H.M. Advocate* (1998)).

In *Drury v. H.M. Advocate* (2001) the accused and the deceased had lived together and, although they were living apart at the time of the killing, it had been accepted at the trial that there was still a relationship between the parties and the accused was entitled to expect sexual fidelity on the part of the deceased. The accused suspected that the deceased had been unfaithful when he saw another man leaving her home. When he confronted her and asked what was going on, she replied "what do you think?" The accused then attacked the deceased, hitting her on the head with a claw hammer and killed her. He was convicted of murder and appealed on the basis that the trial judge had misdirected the jury that there must be a "reasonable relationship" between the provocation offered and the violence used by the accused. Lord Justice-General

Rodger stated (at p. 597) that the trial judge was wrong to give that direction since "the sexual activity and the appellant's attack on the deceased are actually incommensurable." He accepted the suggestion by the appellant's counsel that the test of proportionality should be rejected and instead the accused's act in killing the deceased would fall to be treated as culpable homicide only if the ordinary man (or woman, as the case may be) would have been liable to act in the same way, in the same circumstances. The appeal was allowed and authority for a new prosecution was granted. At the subsequent trial *H.M. Advocate v. Drury* (unreported, August 2001, Edinburgh High Court) the accused was again charged with murder and pled provocation and diminished responsibility (relying on the decision in *Galbraith v. H.M. Advocate* (2001), referred to above). The jury returned a verdict of guilty of murder.

Intoxication

The general rule is that voluntary intoxication is not a defence to a criminal act. In *H.M. Advocate v. Savage* (1923) Lord Justice-Clerk Alness directed the jury, at (pp. 50–51):

"[T]o say that a man, who takes a drink and while under its influence commits a crime, is to be excused from the penalty of the crime merely because he made himself drunk would of course be a most perilous doctrine. And it is not the law of Scotland. The man himself is responsible for getting drunk, and the mere fact that he has taken drink, and while under its influence committed a crime, is not sufficient to excuse him from the consequences of his crime."

In *Ross v. H.M. Advocate* (1991) the court stated:

"[W]here the condition which has resulted in an absence of *mens rea* is self-induced ... the accused must be assumed to have intended the natural consequences of his act."

Note that, although voluntary intoxication is not a formal defence it would be referred to in a plea in mitigation.

The situation of involuntary intoxication is clearly different. In *H.M. Advocate v. Raiker* (1989) Lord McCluskey said an accused would lack the criminal state of mind that is a necessary ingredient of any crime where he had acted wholly and completely under the influence of some drug which was administered by force or without his consent.

Necessity

The defence of necessity is used where the accused behaves in a manner which is not legal to avoid another danger. This defence is often used, therefore, where the accused has been coerced by circumstances into breaking the law. The High Court has been willing to recognise this defence, despite Hume's disapproval (i, 54–55), but there are strict requirements presumably to avoid the defence being used in frivolous circumstances.

Recent cases have tended to concentrate on road traffic offences. In *Tudhope v. Grubb* (1983) the accused paid another man £75 in advance to repair his car. Three months later the repairs had not been carried out and the accused, after six pints of beer, went to visit the man. An argument started and the man and two of his friends assaulted the accused. The accused escaped from the men and got into his car which was attacked by the men kicking it and trying to smash the windows. He then tried to drive off in his car but the battery was flat so it wouldn't start. The police arrived and the accused was charged with attempting to drive with an excess of alcohol in his blood. The sheriff held that the accused had attempted to drive in an effort to save himself further injury and that he had made a full disclosure of the facts to the police at the first available opportunity. Finding the defence of necessity established the accused was acquitted.

In subsequent cases, where the accused is deemed to have other courses of action available to her, the defence has not been available. In *Moss v. Howdle* (1997) the accused was convicted of speeding on a motorway. He claimed that he thought his passenger was seriously ill and drove to the nearest service station where the passenger told him he was only suffering from an attack of cramp. The sheriff accepted that, in the circumstances, it was reasonable to suspect that the passenger was seriously ill but said that the accused should have found out what was wrong with the passenger, by stopping at the side of the road, before he committed the offence. As another course of action was available, the defence of necessity was not available. On appeal, the Court held that the defence of necessity would be available in respect of medical emergencies as well as to avoid violent attacks so long as there was an immediate danger of death or great bodily harm (this is a requirement of both coercion and self-defence). The Court also stated that the defence was available to protect a third party, but was not available to the accused in this particular case because an alternative course of action was available to him which did not involve committing an offence. The appeal was refused.

The strict requirements of the necessity defence are also illustrated in *Ruxton v. Lang* (1998) where a woman, who was threatened by her boyfriend with a knife, drove from her home in a car with excess alcohol in her blood. The sheriff held that while the defence of necessity was available to a charge of driving with excess alcohol it was not available to the accused in this case. In his note to the Appeal Court, the sheriff stated that necessity requires that the accused is still acting under duress of circumstances at the time the crime is committed. The sheriff was of the view that the accused could have stopped her car as soon as the danger had ceased to exist. When the police stopped her, in the locality of her brother's house, this was deemed to be the point at which the offence was committed, however, the sheriff determined that the danger had ceased to exist before this time. The defence agent submitted that it would not have been advisable for his client to get out of her car and walk in the early hours of the morning to her brother's house. However, the sheriff stated that, in the absence of evidence about the locality, he was unable to make such a finding. The accused was convicted and leave to appeal was refused.

Superior Orders

A soldier or policeman may have a defence of superior orders, provided he acted within the rules of service and in pursuit of a legal aim (*H.M. Advocate v. Sheppard* (1941)).

Entrapment

There is no defence of entrapment in Scots law. If evidence of crime is improperly obtained by the police it may be inadmissible. In addition, the fact that the police may have encouraged the commission of a crime may be relevant to sentence, if not to guilt.

READING

P. W. Ferguson, *Crimes Against the Person* (2nd ed., Butterworths, Edinburgh, 1998), Chaps 9–11, 13.

C. Gane, C. Stoddart and J. Chalmers, *A Casebook on Scottish Criminal Law* (3rd ed., W. Green & Son, Edinburgh, 2001), Chaps 7, 10.

G. H. Gordon, *Criminal Law* (3rd ed., M. Christie (ed.), W. Green & Son, Edinburgh, 2000), Vol. I, Chaps 10–13.

T. Jones and M. Christie, *Criminal Law* (2nd ed., W. Green & Son, Edinburgh, 1996), Chaps 8 and 9.

R. McCall Smith and D. Sheldon, *Scots Criminal Law* (Butterworths, Edinburgh, 1997), Chaps 8, 10.

APPENDIX 1: SAMPLE QUESTIONS

QUESTION WITH FULL ANSWER

Question 1

Bob operates a wheel-clamping service on behalf of local businesses. One Friday morning he is called out by Chris, the manager of a local toy shop, who is furious that a car has been parked in their delivery bay, preventing access to the shop. Bob clamps the car and sticks a notice on the windscreen saying that the clamp will be removed on the payment of a £50 fine. Bob then goes to see David the local butcher who wants something to be done about a motorcycle that has been left in front of his shop window. Bob is unable to fit the clamp to the motorcycle, so using a winch on his truck drags it around the corner and parks it in an alleyway behind the shop. After work he goes to an electrical goods store where a friend of his, Eric, works. He tells Eric that he is short of money but would like to purchase a stereo costing £350. He says he will write a cheque, and asks Brian to circumvent the normal shop procedures for checking that the customer has the money in their bank account. Eric agrees to do this, and tells the manager that he has gone through the procedure when he has not in fact done so. Bob leaves the shop with the stereo.

Discuss the criminal liability of Bob and Eric.

Answer

When Bob clamps the wheel of the car he has intentionally appropriated another person's property without their consent (the *mens rea* and *actus reus* of theft). Appropriation of property does not require that it is taken away. In this case appropriation is fulfilled as the clamping of the car deprives the owner of the use and possession of their property. The *mens rea* of intention can be inferred from Bob's actions. He should be charged with theft. Contrary to Hume's traditional definition of theft, which required an intention to permanently deprive, clandestine taking of another person's property aimed at achieving a nefarious purpose is sufficient for theft. This has also been referred to as holding property to ransom, e.g. Bob clamping a car until payment is made (*Milne v. Tudhope* (1981); *Kidston v. Annan* (1984)). However, even where there is not a nefarious purpose, an intention to deprive the owner temporarily of their property has been held to be sufficient for the law of theft (*Black v. Carmichael*; *Carmichael v. Black* (1992)).

Bob should be charged with an alternative crime of attempted extortion for placing the notice on the windscreen demanding money. Extortion has a *mens rea* of intention and the *actus reus* is a threat accompanied by a demand. In this instance, the threat is the refusal to remove the wheel clamp, until payment of the demand of £50. As the demand has not been met the relevant charge is attempted extortion (*Black v. Carmichael*; *Carmichael v. Black* (1992)).

As regards the movement of the motorcycle, Bob's intention to deprive the owner of their property can be inferred from his failed attempt to "clamp" the motorcycle and the movement of the motorcycle to the alleyway behind the shop. Temporary deprivation arising from property being left where the owner is not liable to discover, by his own investigations, was held to be sufficient for a sheriff to draw the inference that the thief had the intention to permanently deprive the owner of a motorcar (*Kivlin v. Milne* (1979)). Case law does not indicate the extent to which an owner must go to recover their property or how long they require to have searched for their property before the actions will amount to theft. It is clear that even when property has been recovered that a charge of theft can be relevant (*Fowler v. O'Brien* (1994)). The fact that there has been no demand for money from the motorcycle owner is irrelevant as the court in *Black v. Carmichael*; *Carmichael v. Black* (1992) held that a nefarious purpose was not necessary and it is the owner's loss and not the other's gain which is important (p. 720). In light of the foregoing, Bob should be charged with theft of the motorcycle.

Bob and Eric should be charged art and part fraud in respect of the purchase of the stereo. They have entered in to a common plan to defraud the shop manager (*H.M. Advocate v. Lappen* (1956)). The *actus reus* of fraud is a false pretence which causes a practical result (*MacDonald v. H.M. Advocate* (1996)). The false pretence is Bob writing the cheque and Eric telling the shop manager that normal procedures have been fulfilled. The practical result is Bob taking away the stereo. The *mens rea* is knowledge that the representation is false and intention to deceive the other party into acting in a way that they would not otherwise have done. Eric and Bob's knowledge of the falsity can be inferred from Bob's declaration that he has no money. Their intention to deceive the shop manager can be inferred from Bob requesting, and Eric agreeing, to tell the shop manager that normal procedures have been fulfilled. In fraud, what matters is the person's present intent as to his future conduct (*Richards v. H.M. Advocate* (1971)). There is no suggestion in the question that Bob intends to lodge adequate funds in his bank account and, therefore, his present intent is to commit fraud. The crime of theft is not relevant here because the stereo is removed with the consent of the owner.

OUTLINE QUESTIONS AND ANSWERS

Question 2
While at a disco at the student union Susan met Brian, a fellow law student. They chatted for a while and Brian asked if Susan would like a drink. She asked for a vodka and fresh orange, explaining that she didn't like the taste of alcohol. Brian ordered an orange alco-pop and asked the bartender to put a double shot of vodka into it. After drinking the vodka

Susan got more chatty and twice insisted on going to the bar to get more drinks. The disco came to an end and Brian offered to walk Susan to the taxi rank. The queue at the rank was very long and Brian suggested they went back to his flat to phone for a taxi. When they reached the flat Brian showed Susan into the lounge and went off to make coffee. When he returned she was lying on the couch asleep. Brian initially lay beside her and later had sexual intercourse with Susan. Brian admits to having "taken advantage" of Susan but says that she must have agreed to have intercourse as she didn't stop him.

Advise the Crown Office on the appropriate charges which should be brought; and advise the accused as to any defences that may be available.

Answer

• The first crime to be considered is rape. The definition of the *actus reus* of rape is "the carnal knowledge of a female person by a male person obtained by force and overcoming her will". The *mens rea* is intention. In respect of the *actus reus*, particular consideration should be given to whether Brian has overcome Susan's will, *i.e.* if the *actus reus* was fulfilled. The *actus reus* can be achieved by drugging or intoxication, however, the accused must have incapacitated the woman with the intention of having intercourse against her will. The fact that Susan voluntarily drank alcohol and whether Brian intended to have intercourse against Susan's will at the time he gave her the drink should be discussed referring to authority (*H.M. Advocate v. Grainger* (1932) *H.M. Advocate v. Logan* (1935)).

• The statutory charge contained within section 7(2)(c) of the Criminal Law (Consolidation) (Scotland) Act 1995, *re* drugging or overcoming a person's will for the purpose of having intercourse, should be considered as an alternative charge. It should be noted that this crime is subject to a maximum punishment of two years' imprisonment and, therefore, conviction of a common law offence could facilitate a longer sentence.

• The alternative charge of clandestine injury when the victim's will is not present and does not require to be overcome should be considered. The *mens rea* and *actus reus* should be considered with reference to cases, *e.g. Charles Sweenie* (1958) and *X v. Sweeney* (1982). The possibility of a conviction of a lesser offence following on a charge of rape should be referred to, Criminal Law (Consolidation) (Scotland) Act 1995, s.14.

• Error and absence of *mens rea* as a result of the honest belief by Brain that Susan had consented should be discussed referring to *Meek v. H.M. Advocate* (1982) and *Jamieson v. H.M. Advocate* (1994). Whether an accused still requires any mistaken belief to be both honest and reasonable, when the charge is indecent assault, should be considered with reference to *Young v. McGlennan* (1991).

Question 3

To what extent is the principle of autonomy—that there should be no liability for actions over which the actor had no control or did not choose to perform—respected by Scots criminal law?

Answer

*   This question requires an outline of the defences available to an accused person who commits a crime but does not have control over their actions when they do so. The principle of autonomy, therefore, extends more widely than just the defence of automatism.
*   The defences that should be considered are: coercion, automatism and insanity.
*   Hume set the following conditions for coercion: there must be an immediate danger of death or great bodily harm; an inability to resist the violence; a backward and inferior part in the perpetration, and a disclosure of the fact, as well as restitution of the spoil, on the first safe and convenient occasion. Reference should be made to *H.M. Advocate v. Thomson,* to discuss how these conditions have been interpreted.
*   Automatism should be discussed with reference to *Cunningham* and *Ross,* where the basic requirements in law before automatism can operate as a defence are outlined. The consequences for an accused who offends while experiencing an epileptic attack or as a result of another "internal" condition should be fully examined as well as those accused who offend while suffering a hypoglycaemic attack (*H.M. Advocate v. Watret* (unreported, Kilmarnock High Court, October 1999)).
*   The requirements of the insanity defence (Hume, i, 37 and *H.M. Advocate v. Kidd* (1960)) should be fully discussed together with the disposals now available to the court when an accused is acquitted on the grounds of insanity (Criminal Procedure (Scotland) Act 1995, s.57).
*   To fully answer this question you must consider whether the principle of autonomy is fully respected. The defences outlined above have very strict requirements that must be fulfilled before the defence is available to an accused. This results in, *e.g.* a person who offends while having an epileptic fit having no defence available unless they also happen to be insane at the time of their offending. A person who kills another under duress cannot use the defence of coercion. Some consideration should also be given to the possible detention in hospital for an accused who is acquitted due to insanity at the time of the offence.

Author's note

These sample questions are adapted from those used in the Criminal Law Ordinary course at the University of Glasgow. The assistance of Professor Lindsay Farmer in drafting these questions, and of Lisa Pearson, Dr Lachlan Bell and Edward McHugh is gratefully acknowledged. The views and any errors expressed in this text are the sole responsibility of the author.

APPENDIX 2: ADDENDUM

Since completion of this text the decision of the Appeal Court in *Lord Advocate's Reference (No. 1 of 2001)* (2002), has changed the definition of the crime of rape. Students are advised to read this decision.

The Lord Advocate's reference arose from the acquittal of a man on a charge of rape. The man had been acquitted by the trial judge who upheld a "no case to answer" submission on the grounds the crime of rape had not been established by the Crown. The trial judge held that for a conviction of rape it was essential that the complainer was subjected to some degree of force or threat or force, and the fact that sexual intercourse took place without her consent was insufficient for conviction. The Lord Advocate submitted and the Appeal Court accepted that the approach of the trial judge correctly reflected the law of rape. The Lord Advocate invited the court to review the law relating to the crime of rape and to hold that the *actus reus* consisted of sexual intercourse by a man with a woman who at the time of the intercourse did not consent to it. The Court held, by majority that:

(1) the *actus reus* of rape is constituted by a man having sexual intercourse with a woman without her consent;

(2) that in the case of females under the age of 12 or who for any other reason are incapable of giving such consent, the absence of consent should, as at present, be presumed; and

(3) the *mens rea* of the crime of rape is present where the man knows the women is not consenting, *i.e.* he acts intentionally or he is reckless as to whether she is consenting. In accordance with the decision in *Jamieson* (1994), recklessness is to be understood in the subjective sense, *i.e.* it requires that the man failed to think about or was indifferent to, whether or not the woman was consenting.

This decision has overruled *Charles Sweenie* (1858). In *Sweenie*, the court held that where intercourse took place without the use of force, *e.g.* where a woman was sleeping, it was not relevant to charge this as rape but clandestine injury. As noted earlier in this text, this approach was also adopted where a man had intercourse with a woman who was insensible due to alcohol, drugs or for any other reason which was not caused by the man. This is now overruled. The fact that the *actus reus* of rape is now intercourse with a woman without her consent means that intercourse with an insensible woman, who is unable to express her consent, should now be treated as rape. The onus of proof remains on the prosecution to prove that the man intended to have intercourse with the woman without her consent or that he was reckless as to whether or not she was consenting.

The Court held that the effect of the court's decision in *Jamieson* (1994) is that a subjective test of recklessness is to be applied in respect of rape. The Court held that consent will be presumed absent in cases involving girls under the age of 12 and those deemed incapable of consenting.

INDEX